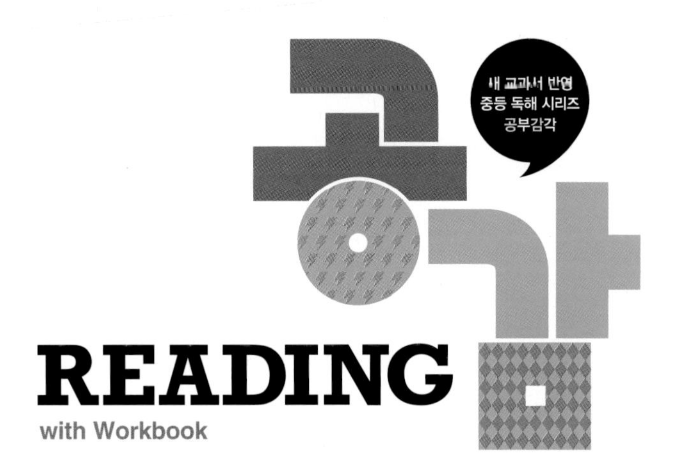


Level 2

**Reading 공감** Level 2

지은이 넥서스영어교육연구소
펴낸이 임상진
펴낸곳 (주)넥서스

출판신고 1992년 4월 3일 제311-2002-2호 ⑤
10880 경기도 파주시 지목로 5
Tel (02)330-5500 Fax (02)330-5555

ISBN 978-89-6790-883-6 54740
978-89-6790-881-2 (SET)



※집필에 도움을 주신 분
:Carolyn Papworth, Minji Kim, Hailey Ma, McKathy Green, Rachel Swan

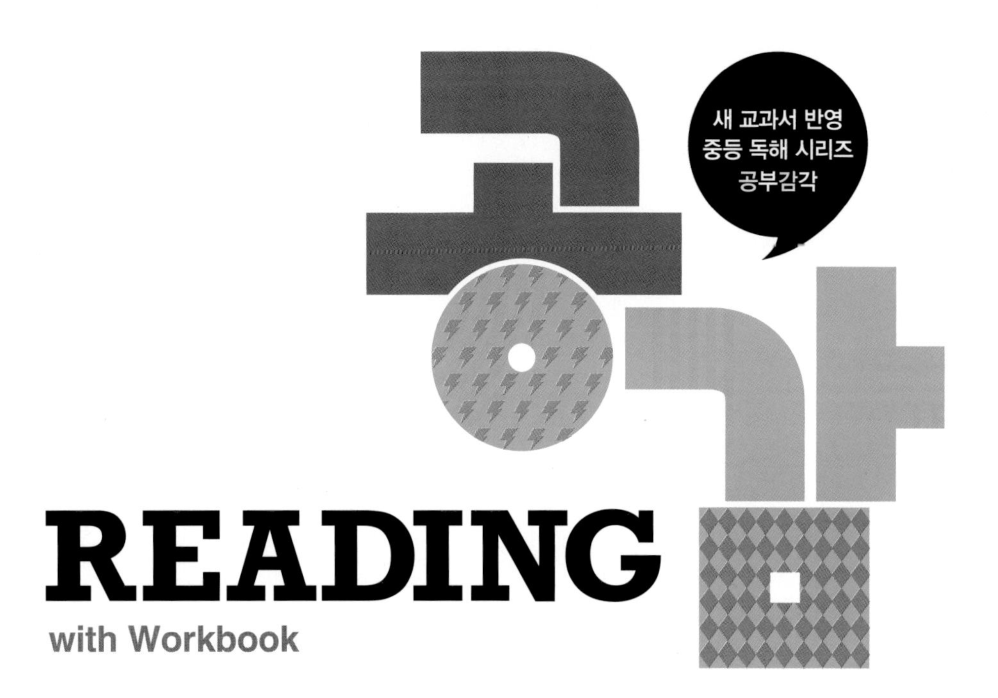


# READING

with Workbook

넥서스영어교육연구소 지음

Level 2

NEXUS Edu

# Reading Gong Gam helps you...

## Get high scores
최신 개정 교과서에 수록된 창의, 나눔, 문화, 건강, 과학, 심리, 음식, 직업 등의 다양한 주제로 독해 지문을 구성하여 영어에 흥미를 가지게 함으로써 내신 성적 향상에 도움을 줍니다.

## Obtain a wide vocabulary
풍부한 어휘 리스트를 제공, 기본적인 어휘 실력을 향상시켜 줍니다.

## Nurture your English skills
최신 개정 교과서를 분석하여 만든 다양한 지문 및 문제로 독해의 기초를 튼튼히 다져 줍니다. 중등 과정에서 알아야 하는 풍부한 어휘를 제공함으로써 종합적인 영어 실력을 향상시켜 줍니다.

## Get writing skills
서술형 평가 문제를 수록하고 서술형 대비 워크북을 따로 제공하여 새로운 교수 평가 방법에 대비할 수 있게 해 줍니다.

## Get speaking skills
이미지맵을 통해 글의 요점과 구조, 흐름을 파악하고 그 정보를 이용하여 스스로 스토리텔링을 해 봄으로써 수행평가에 대비하고, 스피킹 능력을 향상시킬 수 있게 해 줍니다.

## Acquire good English sense
풍부한 양의 영어 지문을 읽어 봄으로써 영어의 기본 감각을 익히고, 이미지맵을 통해 영어식 사고의 흐름을 파악할 수 있게 해 줍니다.

## Master the essentials of reading
엄선된 지문과 문제, 풍부한 어휘, 다양한 배경지식 등을 통해 영어 이해의 필수 요소인 독해를 정복할 수 있게 해 줍니다.

## 다양한 주제의 지문

최신 교과서에 수록된 창의, 나눔, 사회, 문화, 건강, 과학, 심리, 음식, 직업, 이슈 등의 주제를 이용하여 흥미롭고 유익한 지문으로 구성하였습니다.

## 객관식·서술형 문제

기본 독해 실력을 확인할 수 있는 내신 대비 유형의 객관식, 서술형 문제로 구성하였습니다.

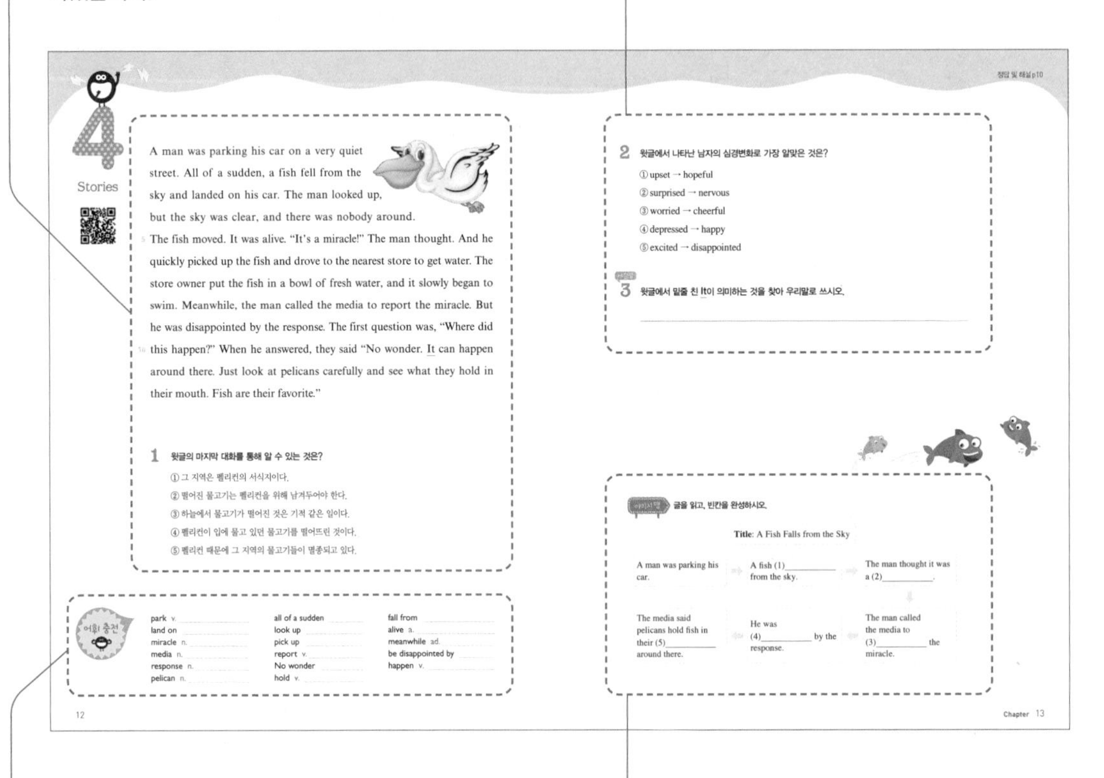

정답 및 해설 p10

4 Stories

A man was parking his car on a very quiet street. All of a sudden, a fish fell from the sky and landed on his car. The man looked up, but the sky was clear, and there was nobody around. The fish moved. It was alive. "It's a miracle!" The man thought. And he quickly picked up the fish and drove to the nearest store to get water. The store owner put the fish in a bowl of fresh water, and it slowly began to swim. Meanwhile, the man called the media to report the miracle. But he was disappointed by the response. The first question was, "Where did this happen?" When he answered, they said "No wonder. It can happen around there. Just look at pelicans carefully and see what they hold in their mouth. Fish are their favorite."

1 윗글의 마지막 대화를 통해 알 수 있는 것은?

① 그 지역은 펠리컨의 서식지이다.
② 떨어진 물고기는 펠리컨을 위해 남겨두어야 한다.
③ 하늘에서 물고기가 떨어진 것은 기적 같은 일이다.
④ 펠리컨이 입에 물고 있던 물고기를 떨어뜨린 것이다.
⑤ 펠리컨 때문에 그 지역의 물고기들이 멸종되고 있다.

어휘 충전

| | | |
|---|---|---|
| park v. | all of a sudden | fall from |
| land on | look up | alive a. |
| miracle n. | pick up | meanwhile ad. |
| media n. | report v. | be disappointed by |
| response n. | No wonder | happen v. |
| pelican n. | hold v. | |

2 윗글에서 나타난 남자의 심경변화로 가장 알맞은 것은?

① upset → hopeful
② surprised → nervous
③ worried → cheerful
④ depressed → happy
⑤ excited → disappointed

서술형
3 윗글에서 밑줄 친 It이 의미하는 것을 찾아 우리말로 쓰시오.

이미지맵 글을 읽고, 빈칸을 완성하시오.

Title: A Fish Falls from the Sky

A man was parking his car. → A fish (1)__________ from the sky. → The man thought it was a (2)__________.

The media said pelicans hold fish in their (5)__________ around there. ← He was (4)__________ by the response. ← The man called the media to (3)__________ the miracle.

12

Chapter 13

## 어휘 충전

독해의 기본은 어휘, 어휘 실력을 먼저 점검해 보고 독해 실력을 향상시키는 코너로 구성하였습니다.

## 이미지맵

독해 지문의 내용을 자연스럽게 스토리텔링 할 수 있도록 단계별로 나누어 체계적으로 요약 정리하였습니다.

지식 채널

**바다 속의 레스토랑**

2005년 3월에 오픈한 몰디브의 이싸(Ithaa) 레스토랑은 깊은 바다 속의 물고기들을 감상하면서 식사를 할 수 있는 해저 레스토랑이다. 해수면 4.87미터 아래 아름다운 산호초 위에 자리잡은 레스토랑은 바닥을 제외한 모든 벽면이 유리로 만들어져서 손님들은 신비한 물 속 세계를 180도 파노라마 전망으로 한눈에 볼 수 있다. 특히 몰디브의 바다는 바다거북이, 초대형 가오리 등 신비하고 특이한 물고기들의 서식지이며, 그 수중환경은 대자연의 경이로움을 그대로 보여주기 때문에 세계 관광객들에게 큰 인기를 끌고 있다.

## 지식 채널

독해 지문과 직접적으로 관련이 있는 배경지식뿐만 아니라, 독해 실력 향상의 기초가 되는 다양한 배경지식을 제공하고 있습니다.

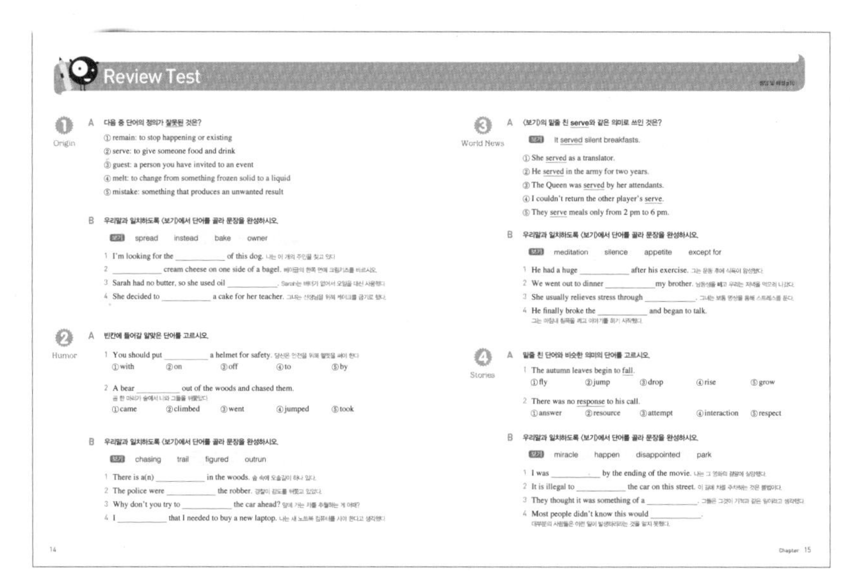
Review Test

1 Origin

A 다음 중 단어의 정의가 잘못된 것은?

① remain: to stop happening or existing
② serve: to give someone food and drink
③ guest: a person you have invited to an event
④ melt: to change from something frozen solid to a liquid
⑤ mistake: something that produces an unwanted result

B 우리말과 일치하도록 〈보기〉에서 단어를 골라 문장을 완성하시오.

보기 spread instead bake owner

1 I'm looking for the ___________ of this dog. 나는 이 개의 주인을 찾고 있다
2 ___________ cream cheese on one side of a bagel. 베이글의 한쪽 면에 크림치즈를 바르시오.
3 Sarah had no butter, so she used oil ___________. Sarah는 버터가 없어서 오일을 대신 사용했다
4 She decided to ___________ a cake for her teacher. 그녀는 선생님을 위해 케이크를 굽기로 했다.

2 Humor

A 빈칸에 들어갈 알맞은 단어를 고르시오.

1 You should put ___________ a helmet for safety. 당신은 안전을 위해 헬멧을 써야 한다
① with ② on ③ off ④ to ⑤ by

2 A bear ___________ out of the woods and chased them.
곰 한 마리가 숲에서 나와 그들을 뒤쫓았다
① came ② climbed ③ went ④ jumped ⑤ took

B 우리말과 일치하도록 〈보기〉에서 단어를 골라 문장을 완성하시오.

보기 chasing trail figured outrun

1 There is a(n) ___________ in the woods. 숲 속에 오솔길이 하나 있다.
2 The police were ___________ the robber. 경찰이 강도를 뒤쫓고 있었다.
3 Why don't you try to ___________ the car ahead? 앞에 가는 차를 추월하는 게 어때?
4 I ___________ that I needed to buy a new laptop. 나는 새 노트북 컴퓨터를 사야 한다고 생각했다

14

3 World News

A 〈보기〉의 밑줄 친 serve와 같은 의미로 쓰인 것은?

보기 It served silent breakfasts.

① She served as a translator.
② He served in the army for two years.
③ The Queen was served by her attendants.
④ I couldn't return the other player's serve.
⑤ They serve meals only from 2 pm to 6 pm.

B 우리말과 일치하도록 〈보기〉에서 단어를 골라 문장을 완성하시오.

보기 meditation silence appetite except for

1 He had a huge ___________ after his exercise. 그는 운동 후에 식욕이 왕성했다
2 We went out to dinner ___________ my brother. 남동생을 빼고 우리는 저녁을 먹으러 나갔다
3 She usually relieves stress through ___________. 그녀는 보통 명상을 통해 스트레스를 푼다
4 He finally broke the ___________ and began to talk.
그는 마침내 침묵을 깨고 이야기를 하기 시작했다.

4 Stories

A 밑줄 친 단어와 비슷한 의미의 단어를 고르시오.

1 The autumn leaves begin to fall.
① fly ② jump ③ drop ④ rise ⑤ grow

2 There was no response to his call.
① answer ② resource ③ attempt ④ interaction ⑤ respect

B 우리말과 일치하도록 〈보기〉에서 단어를 골라 문장을 완성하시오.

보기 miracle happen disappointed park

1 I was ___________ by the ending of the movie. 나는 그 영화의 결말에 실망했다
2 It is illegal to ___________ the car on this street. 이 길에 차를 주차하는 것은 불법이다.
3 They thought it was something of a ___________. 그들은 그것이 기적과 같은 일이라고 생각했다
4 Most people didn't know this would ___________.
대부분의 사람들은 이런 일이 발생하리라는 것을 알지 못했다.

Chapter 15

## Review Test

영영풀이, 유의어, 반의어, 다의어 등을 묻는 문제와 빈칸 채우기 문제를 통해 어휘를 복습할 수 있도록 구성하였습니다.

## 어휘 재충전

어휘 충전 코너에 없는 우리말 뜻을 제공하여 어휘의 의미를 쉽게 확인할 수 있도록 구성하였습니다.

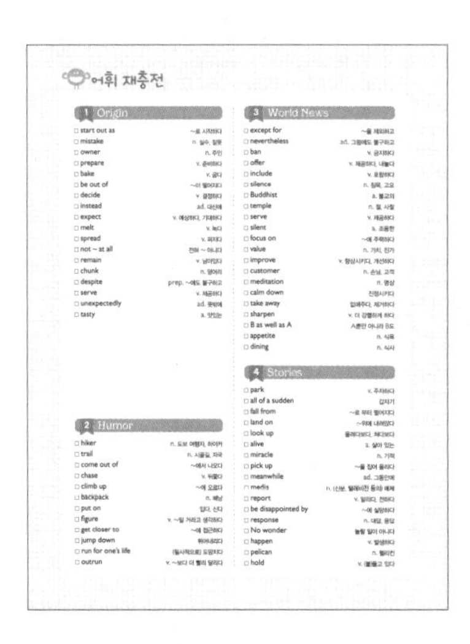

## Workbook

서술형 대비 워크북을 통해 어휘 및 문장 배열, 쓰기 문제를 마스터 할 수 있도록 구성하였습니다.

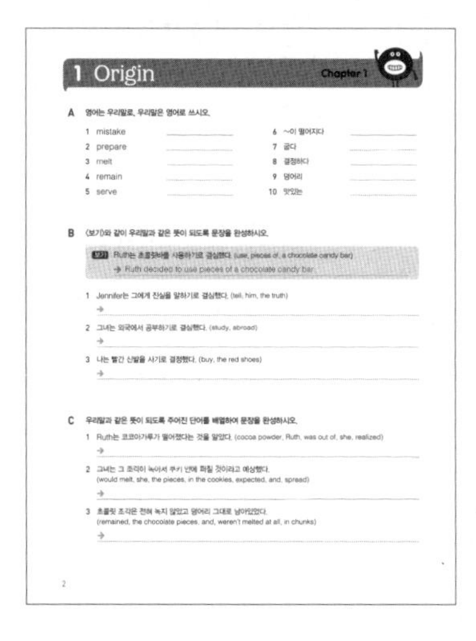

## Answers

어휘, 중요 구문 분석을 통해 정확하고 명쾌한 해설을 확인할 수 있습니다.

# Contents

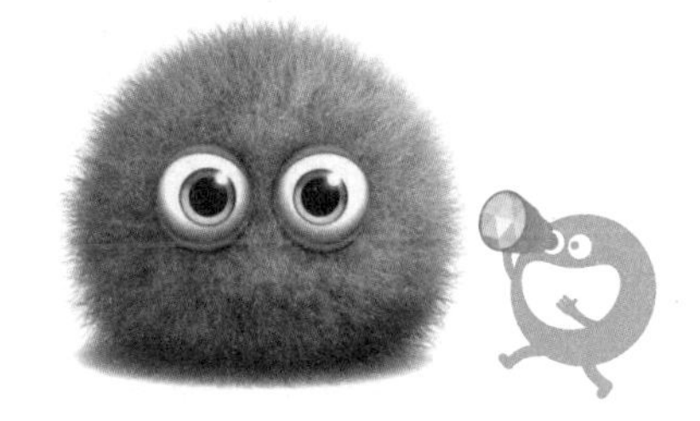

# Chapter 01

# Origin

America's best-loved cookie actually started out as a mistake. Ruth Wakefield was the owner of the Toll House Inn in Massachusetts in the 1930s. One day, when Ruth was preparing to bake chocolate cookies for her guests, she realized she was out of cocoa powder. So Ruth decided to use pieces of a chocolate candy bar instead. She expected the pieces would melt and spread in the cookies as they baked in the oven. But she was wrong. The chocolate pieces weren't melted at all and remained in chunks. Despite this, she had to serve them. Unexpectedly, the guests loved them. This is how we got tasty chocolate chip cookies.

**1** Ruth Wakefield에 관한 윗글의 내용과 일치하지 않는 것은?

① Toll House Inn의 주인이었다.
② 1930년대 메사추세츠에서 살았다.
③ 초콜릿 칩 쿠키를 최초로 만든 사람이다.
④ 우연히 초콜릿 칩 쿠키를 만들었다.
⑤ 초콜릿 바 조각들이 녹지 않을 거라고 예상했다.

**2** Ruth Wakefield가 쿠키에 초콜릿 바를 넣은 이유로 가장 알맞은 것은?

① 코코아 가루가 떨어져서 ② 새로운 메뉴 개발을 위해 ③ 손님이 주문해서
④ 실수로 상표를 잘못 봐서 ⑤ 초콜릿 맛 쿠키가 먹고 싶어서

| | | |
|---|---|---|
| start out as ______ | mistake n. ______ | owner n. ______ |
| prepare v. ______ | bake v. ______ | be out of ______ |
| decide v. ______ | instead ad. ______ | expect v. ______ |
| melt v. ______ | spread v. ______ | not ~ at all ______ |
| remain v. ______ | chunk n. ______ | despite prep. ______ |
| serve v. ______ | unexpectedly ad. ______ | tasty a. ______ |

Two hikers are walking along a trail. Suddenly, a bear comes out of the woods and starts chasing them. They quickly climb up a tree, but (climbing, starts, the bear, after, them). The first hiker gets his sneakers out of his backpack and puts them on. The second hiker says, "What are you doing?" The first hiker says, "I figure that when the bear gets closer to us, we'll jump down and run for our lives." The second hiker says, "Are you crazy? You can't outrun a bear!" The first hiker says, "I don't have to outrun the bear. I only have to outrun you!"

**1** 윗글의 마지막 말을 통해 알 수 있는 것은?

① 두 여행자는 곰을 사냥할 것이다.
② 두 번째 여행자는 달리기를 잘 할 것이다.
③ 첫 번째 여행자는 곰과 격투를 벌일 것이다.
④ 첫 번째 여행자는 혼자서 도망칠 것이다.
⑤ 두 번째 여행자는 첫 번째 여행자와 달리기 경주를 할 것이다.

서술형
**2** 윗글의 ( ) 안에 주어진 단어를 우리말에 맞게 배열하여 문장을 완성하시오.

그 곰은 그들을 따라 올라오기 시작했다.

_______________________________________________

| | | |
|---|---|---|
| hiker n. ________ | trail n. ________ | come out of ________ |
| chase v. ________ | climb up ________ | backpack n. ________ |
| put on ________ | figure v. ________ | get closer to ________ |
| jump down ________ | run for one's life ________ | outrun v. ________ |

World News

Except for eating good food, what do most people like to do in restaurants? They like to have a good conversation with friends. Nevertheless, there's one New York restaurant where talking is banned. Why? Once a week, this popular New York restaurant offers a special set menu for $40. The dinner includes four courses and one rule — total silence. "I got the idea from a Buddhist temple I stayed at," said the owner. "It served silent breakfasts to teach people to focus on the taste and health value of the food." He said it improved his whole experience of eating. Now, many customers agree. "It's like meditation," one said. "It calms down my busy mind and takes away stress." It seems that it could sharpen our minds as well as our appetites!

| | | |
|---|---|---|
| except for ______ | nevertheless ad. ______ | ban v. ______ |
| offer v. ______ | include v. ______ | silence n. ______ |
| Buddhist a. ______ | temple n. ______ | serve v. ______ |
| silent a. ______ | focus on ______ | value n. ______ |
| improve v. ______ | customer n. ______ | meditation n. ______ |
| calm down ______ | take away ______ | sharpen v. ______ |
| B as well as A ______ | appetite n. ______ | dining n. ______ |

**1** 윗글의 제목으로 가장 알맞은 것은?

① Strange Restaurants in the World
② The Best Restaurant in New York
③ Silent Dining at a Buddhist Temple
④ A Restaurant Where Silence Is Golden
⑤ How to Start Conversation with a Stranger

**2** 레스토랑에 관한 윗글의 내용과 일치하지 않는 것은?

① 뉴욕에 위치해 있다.
② 한 달에 한 번 특별 세트 메뉴를 제공한다.
③ 특별 세트 메뉴에는 4가지 코스요리가 포함되어 있다.
④ 특별 세트 메뉴를 먹을 때는 대화를 할 수 없다.
⑤ 특별 세트 메뉴는 40달러이다.

**3** 윗글에서 다음 질문에 대한 답을 찾아 우리말로 쓰시오.

Where did the owner get the idea?

______________________________

**바다 속의 레스토랑**

2005년 3월에 오픈한 몰디브의 이싸(Ithaa) 레스토랑은 깊은 바다 속의 물고기들을 감상하면서 식사를 할 수 있는 해저 레스토랑이다. 해수면 4.87미터 아래 아름다운 산호초 위에 자리잡은 레스토랑은 바닥을 제외한 모든 벽면이 유리로 만들어져서 손님들은 신비한 물 속 세계를 180도 파노라마 전망으로 한눈에 볼 수 있다. 특히 몰디브의 바다는 바다거북이, 초대형 가오리 등 신비하고 특이한 물고기들의 서식지이며, 그 수중환경은 대자연의 경이로움을 그대로 보여주기 때문에 세계 관광객들에게 큰 인기를 끌고 있다.

Stories

A man was parking his car on a very quiet street. All of a sudden, a fish fell from the sky and landed on his car. The man looked up, but the sky was clear, and there was nobody around. The fish moved. It was alive. "It's a miracle!" The man thought. And he quickly picked up the fish and drove to the nearest store to get water. The store owner put the fish in a bowl of fresh water, and it slowly began to swim. Meanwhile, the man called the media to report the miracle. But he was disappointed by the response. The first question was, "Where did this happen?" When he answered, they said "No wonder. It can happen around there. Just look at pelicans carefully and see what they hold in their mouth. Fish are their favorite."

**1** 윗글의 마지막 대화를 통해 알 수 있는 것은?

① 그 지역은 펠리컨의 서식지이다.
② 떨어진 물고기는 펠리컨을 위해 남겨두어야 한다.
③ 하늘에서 물고기가 떨어진 것은 기적 같은 일이다.
④ 펠리컨이 입에 물고 있던 물고기를 떨어뜨린 것이다.
⑤ 펠리컨 때문에 그 지역의 물고기들이 멸종되고 있다.

| | | |
|---|---|---|
| park v. ________ | all of a sudden ________ | fall from ________ |
| land on ________ | look up ________ | alive a. ________ |
| miracle n. ________ | pick up ________ | meanwhile ad. ________ |
| media n. ________ | report v. ________ | be disappointed by ________ |
| response n. ________ | No wonder ________ | happen v. ________ |
| pelican n. ________ | hold v. ________ | |

**2** 윗글에 나타난 남자의 심경변화로 가장 알맞은 것은?

① upset → hopeful

② surprised → nervous

③ worried → cheerful

④ depressed → happy

⑤ excited → disappointed

**3** 윗글에서 밑줄 친 It이 의미하는 것을 찾아 우리말로 쓰시오.

______________________________

글을 읽고, 빈칸을 완성하시오.

**Title**: A Fish Falls from the Sky

| | | |
|---|---|---|
| A man was parking his car. → | A fish (1)__________ from the sky. → | The man thought it was a (2)__________. ↓ |
| The media said pelicans hold fish in their (5)__________ around there. | ← He was (4)__________ by the response. | ← The man called the media to (3)__________ the miracle. |

# Review Test

## 1 Origin

**A** 다음 중 단어의 정의가 잘못된 것은?

① remain: to stop happening or existing
② serve: to give someone food and drink
③ guest: a person you have invited to an event
④ melt: to change from something frozen solid to a liquid
⑤ mistake: something that produces an unwanted result

**B** 우리말과 일치하도록 〈보기〉에서 단어를 골라 문장을 완성하시오.

보기 spread instead bake owner

1 I'm looking for the ____________ of this dog. 나는 이 개의 주인을 찾고 있다.
2 ____________ cream cheese on one side of a bagel. 베이글의 한쪽 면에 크림치즈를 바르시오.
3 Sarah had no butter, so she used oil ____________. Sarah는 버터가 없어서 오일을 대신 사용했다.
4 She decided to ____________ a cake for her teacher. 그녀는 선생님을 위해 케이크를 굽기로 했다.

## 2 Humor

**A** 빈칸에 들어갈 알맞은 단어를 고르시오.

1 You should put ____________ a helmet for safety. 당신은 안전을 위해 헬멧을 써야 한다.
① with ② on ③ off ④ to ⑤ by

2 A bear ____________ out of the woods and chased them.
곰 한 마리가 숲에서 나와 그들을 뒤쫓았다.
① came ② climbed ③ went ④ jumped ⑤ took

**B** 우리말과 일치하도록 〈보기〉에서 단어를 골라 문장을 완성하시오.

보기 chasing trail figured outrun

1 There is a(n) ____________ in the woods. 숲 속에 오솔길이 하나 있다.
2 The police were ____________ the robber. 경찰이 강도를 뒤쫓고 있었다.
3 Why don't you try to ____________ the car ahead? 앞에 가는 차를 추월하는 게 어때?
4 I ____________ that I needed to buy a new laptop. 나는 새 노트북 컴퓨터를 사야 한다고 생각했다.

정답 및 해설 p3

## 3 World News

**A** 〈보기〉의 밑줄 친 serve와 같은 의미로 쓰인 것은?

보기 It served silent breakfasts.

① She served as a translator.
② He served in the army for two years.
③ The Queen was served by her attendants.
④ I couldn't return the other player's serve.
⑤ They serve meals only from 2 pm to 6 pm.

**B** 우리말과 일치하도록 〈보기〉에서 단어를 골라 문장을 완성하시오.

보기 meditation silence appetite except for

1 He had a huge ____________ after his exercise. 그는 운동 후에 식욕이 왕성했다.
2 We went out to dinner ____________ my brother. 남동생을 빼고 우리는 저녁을 먹으러 나갔다.
3 She usually relieves stress through ____________. 그녀는 보통 명상을 통해 스트레스를 푼다.
4 He finally broke the ____________ and began to talk.
그는 마침내 침묵을 깨고 이야기를 하기 시작했다.

## 4 Stories

**A** 밑줄 친 단어와 비슷한 의미의 단어를 고르시오.

1 The autumn leaves begin to fall.
① fly ② jump ③ drop ④ rise ⑤ grow

2 There was no response to his call.
① answer ② resource ③ attempt ④ interaction ⑤ respect

**B** 우리말과 일치하도록 〈보기〉에서 단어를 골라 문장을 완성하시오.

보기 miracle happen disappointed park

1 I was ____________ by the ending of the movie. 나는 그 영화의 결말에 실망했다.
2 It is illegal to ____________ the car on this street. 이 길에 차를 주차하는 것은 불법이다.
3 They thought it was something of a ____________. 그들은 그것이 기적과 같은 일이라고 생각했다.
4 Most people didn't know this would ____________.
대부분의 사람들은 이런 일이 발생하리라는 것을 알지 못했다.

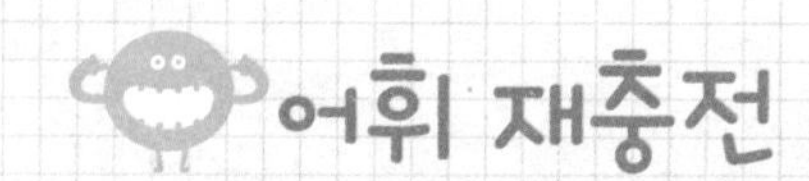

# 어휘 재충전

## 1 Origin

| | |
|---|---|
| □ start out as | ~로 시작하다 |
| □ mistake | n. 실수, 잘못 |
| □ owner | n. 주인 |
| □ prepare | v. 준비하다 |
| □ bake | v. 굽다 |
| □ be out of | ~이 떨어지다 |
| □ decide | v. 결정하다 |
| □ instead | ad. 대신에 |
| □ expect | v. 예상하다, 기대하다 |
| □ melt | v. 녹다 |
| □ spread | v. 퍼지다 |
| □ not ~ at all | 전혀 ~ 아니다 |
| □ remain | v. 남아있다 |
| □ chunk | n. 덩어리 |
| □ despite | prep. ~에도 불구하고 |
| □ serve | v. 제공하다 |
| □ unexpectedly | ad. 뜻밖에 |
| □ tasty | a. 맛있는 |

## 2 Humor

| | |
|---|---|
| □ hiker | n. 도보 여행자, 하이커 |
| □ trail | n. 시골길, 자국 |
| □ come out of | ~에서 나오다 |
| □ chase | v. 뒤쫓다 |
| □ climb up | ~에 오르다 |
| □ backpack | n. 배낭 |
| □ put on | 입다, 신다 |
| □ figure | v. ~일 거라고 생각하다 |
| □ get closer to | ~에 접근하다 |
| □ jump down | 뛰어내리다 |
| □ run for one's life | (필사적으로) 도망치다 |
| □ outrun | v. ~보다 더 빨리 달리다 |

## 3 World News

| | |
|---|---|
| □ except for | ~을 제외하고 |
| □ nevertheless | ad. 그럼에도 불구하고 |
| □ ban | v. 금지하다 |
| □ offer | v. 제공하다, 내놓다 |
| □ include | v. 포함하다 |
| □ silence | n. 침묵, 고요 |
| □ Buddhist | a. 불교의 |
| □ temple | n. 절, 사찰 |
| □ serve | v. 제공하다 |
| □ silent | a. 조용한 |
| □ focus on | ~에 주력하다 |
| □ value | n. 가치, 진가 |
| □ improve | v. 향상시키다, 개선하다 |
| □ customer | n. 손님, 고객 |
| □ meditation | n. 명상 |
| □ calm down | 진정시키다 |
| □ take away | 없애주다, 제거하다 |
| □ sharpen | v. 더 강렬하게 하다 |
| □ B as well as A | A뿐만 아니라 B도 |
| □ appetite | n. 식욕 |
| □ dining | n. 식사 |

## 4 Stories

| | |
|---|---|
| □ park | v. 주차하다 |
| □ all of a sudden | 갑자기 |
| □ fall from | ~로부터 떨어지다 |
| □ land on | ~위에 내려앉다 |
| □ look up | 올려다보다, 쳐다보다 |
| □ alive | a. 살아 있는 |
| □ miracle | n. 기적 |
| □ pick up | ~을 집어 올리다 |
| □ meanwhile | ad. 그동안에 |
| □ media | n. (신문, 텔레비전 등의) 매체 |
| □ report | v. 알리다, 전하다 |
| □ be disappointed by | ~에 실망하다 |
| □ response | n. 대답, 응답 |
| □ no wonder | 놀랄 일이 아니다 |
| □ happen | v. 발생하다 |
| □ pelican | n. 펠리컨 |
| □ hold | v. (붙)들고 있다 |

# Chapter 02

Food

This is one of the world's most delicious foods, but it smells terrible. Say hello to stinky tofu, Taiwan's famous snack. People line up at stinky tofu stands all over Taiwan. There, tofu is deep fried until it's golden and crispy on the outside. Then it's served with a spicy sauce of vinegar, sesame oil, pickled cabbage, and cucumber. It looks delicious. So why does it stink so badly? The answer is fermentation. Before cooking, the tofu is soaked in six-month-old broth made from fermenting meat, milk, fish, and vegetables. Most recipes are secrets. What nobody can hide is the terrible smell. If you dare to try stinky tofu, ______________________________.

*stinky tofu 취두부 *fermentation 발효(작용)

서술형

**1** 윗글에서 알맞은 말을 찾아 다음 요약문을 완성하시오.

> Stinky tofu is one of the famous snacks in Taiwan.
> It smells ____________ because of fermentation.

**2** 윗글의 빈칸에 들어갈 말로 가장 알맞은 것은?

① find the secret recipe ② check the price of it ③ just follow your nose
④ start a new business ⑤ ask your mom for help

| | | |
|---|---|---|
| terrible a. ________ | line up ________ | stand n. ________ |
| all over ________ | golden a. ________ | crispy a. ________ |
| be served with ________ | spicy a. ________ | vinegar n. ________ |
| sesame oil n. ________ | pickled a. ________ | cabbage n. ________ |
| cucumber n. ________ | stink v. ________ | badly ad. ________ |
| soak v. ________ | broth n. ________ | recipe n. ________ |
| hide v. ________ | dare to ________ | |

The vending machine is a great invention. You can find one nearly everywhere, so you're never far away from cold drinks and yummy snacks. In addition, vending machines can sell much more than hot coffee and soda pop. Just look at Japan, for instance. It has the world's most vending machines and some of the strangest ones, too. There are vending machines for fresh eggs, 10 kg bags of rice, fried chicken, hot ramen, and many more foods. There's even a lettuce vending machine. Lettuce plants grow inside the machine, under lights. People all over the world keep inventing new vending machines. Imagine that you can make your own vending machine. What does it look like? How does it work? And what kind of things does it sell?

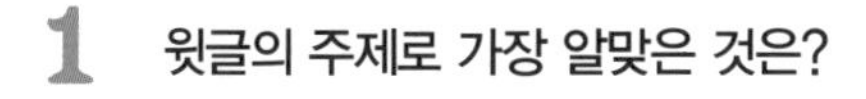

**1** 윗글의 주제로 가장 알맞은 것은?

① why people like vending machines
② how vending machines are invented
③ growing demands of vending machines
④ many different kinds of vending machines
⑤ the importance of vending machines

**2** 윗글에서 자동판매기의 구체적인 판매 품목으로 언급되지 않은 것은?

① 탄산음료　② 달걀　③ 라면
④ 상추　⑤ 책

| | | |
|---|---|---|
| vending machine n. ______ | invention n. ______ | nearly ad. ______ |
| far away ______ | yummy a. ______ | soda pop ______ |
| look at ______ | even ad. ______ | lettuce n. ______ |
| inside prep. ______ | imagine v. ______ | own a. ______ |
| work v. ______ | demand n. ______ | |

Life

Tornadoes are so scary. They happen so suddenly. And you never know which way they will turn or how big they will get. But you can survive them. ① You just need a bit of luck and the following advice. ② There are many different types of tornadoes. ③ As soon as there is a tornado warning sound, go straight to your basement. ④ If you don't have one, then go to a room without windows. ⑤ This is important because broken glass and flying objects are the biggest killers in strong winds. A bathroom is best. Grab blankets or pillows to cover your head. If you're outdoors, find the deepest hollow in the ground near you. Then, lie face down in the hollow. This will protect you a little from flying objects. It might even save you from being sucked up. Let's hope you never need this advice!

| | | |
|---|---|---|
| tornado n. ______ | happen v. ______ | turn v. ______ |
| survive v. ______ | a bit of ______ | following a. ______ |
| advice n. ______ | as soon as ______ | warning sound ______ |
| basement n. ______ | broken a. ______ | object n. ______ |
| grab v. ______ | pillow n. ______ | cover v. ______ |
| hollow n. ______ | lie face down ______ | protect A from B ______ |
| save v. ______ | suck up ______ | |

**1** 윗글에서 토네이도가 왔을 때 취해야 할 행동으로 언급된 것이 아닌 것은?

① 지하실로 가라.

② 담요로 머리를 덮어라.

③ 창문이 없는 방으로 가라.

④ 움푹 패인 구멍 안에 엎드려라.

⑤ 집에 있는 물건을 모두 바닥으로 옮겨라.

**2** 윗글의 밑줄 친 ①~⑤ 중 글의 흐름과 관계가 없는 것은?

① ② ③ ④ ⑤

**3** 윗글에서 밑줄 친 This가 의미하는 것을 찾아 우리말로 쓰시오.

______________________________

**토네이도(Tornado)**

토네이도란 평야나 바다에서 발생하는 강력한 회오리바람의 일종이다. 때때로 트위스터(twister) 또는 사이클론(cyclone)으로 불리기도 한다. 수평 방향의 규모보다 수직 방향의 규모가 크며, 주로 미국 대평원지역에서 발생한다. 토네이도의 모양과 크기는 다양하지만, 보통 깔때기 모양이며 지름은 평균 150 ~ 600 m이고 시속 40 ~ 80 km의 속도로 움직인다. 토네이도의 정확한 형성 원인은 아직 밝혀지지 않았으나, 현재까지의 연구 결과에 따르면 고온 다습한 공기가 불안정한 환경에서 상승할 때 형성되는 것으로 추측되고 있다.

Opinion

Everyone knows that good friends are very important. But what makes a friend a true friend? Let's see what Cathy and Justin think about it.

**Justin**: I thought Josh was my best friend. Now I don't! Yesterday I texted him and asked him to hang out with me. He texted back and said 5 he was busy helping his dad. But I found out today he was hanging out with other friends. He lied to me! A true friend wouldn't do that!

**Cathy**: Yeah. That's pretty bad. Best friends shouldn't lie to each other. Then again, nobody's perfect, right? Even best friends make mistakes. What if Josh didn't want to hurt your feelings? What if that's why he said 10 he was with his dad? You two have been friends for years, so maybe you should forget about it this time. After all, a true friend wouldn't break up with you for one bad mistake. Just try talking to him. You can work it out.

| | | |
|---|---|---|
| text v. ______ | ask v. ______ | hang out with ______ |
| be busy -ing ______ | find out ______ | lie v. ______ |
| nobody ______ | even ad. ______ | make a mistake ______ |
| what if ~? ______ | hurt v. ______ | for years ______ |
| once ad. ______ | after all ______ | break up with ______ |
| work it out ______ | | |

**1** 윗글에서 Justin이 Josh에게 느꼈을 감정으로 가장 알맞은 것은?

① 두려움 ② 걱정스러움 ③ 만족스러움
④ 설렘 ⑤ 실망감

**2** 윗글의 내용과 일치하면 T, 그렇지 않으면 F를 쓰시오.

(1) Josh는 Justin에게 상처를 주지 않으려고 거짓말을 했다. ________
(2) Justin과 Josh는 수년 동안 친구로 지내왔다. ________
(3) Cathy는 Justin에게 Josh와 친하게 지내지 말라고 조언했다. ________

서술형
**3** 윗글에서 밑줄 친 one bad mistake가 의미하는 것을 찾아 우리말로 쓰시오.

________________________________________

이미지 맵 글을 읽고, 빈칸을 완성하시오.

**Title**: Who Is a True Friend?

- Justin
  - True friends shouldn't lie to (1)______________.
- Cathy
  - Best friends make (2)______________.
  - A true friend wouldn't (3)______________ up with his friend for one bad mistake.

# Review Test

## 1 Food

**A** 다음 중 단어의 정의가 잘못된 것은?

① terrible: extremely bad or horrible
② hide: to make something or someone stay
③ recipe: a set of instructions for making food
④ stand: a table used for selling or showing things
⑤ stink: to have a strong and very unpleasant smell

**B** 우리말과 일치하도록 <보기>에서 단어를 골라 문장을 완성하시오.

보기 lined up crispy badly soak

1 I love a ____________ apple pie. 나는 바삭바삭한 사과 파이를 매우 좋아한다.
2 The homeless ____________ need help in winter. 노숙자들은 겨울에 도움이 꼭 필요하다.
3 ____________ the vegetables in cold water for a while. 얼마 동안은 채소를 찬 물에 담가놓아라.
4 People ____________ in front of the famous restaurant.
사람들이 그 유명한 식당 앞에 줄을 서 있었다.

## 2 Culture

**A** 밑줄 친 단어와 반대되는 의미의 단어를 고르시오.

1 Use fresh vegetables and fruits to make juice.
① raw ② natural ③ new ④ old ⑤ pure

2 If you keep doing it, you will be the greatest player.
① break ② call ③ talk ④ pull ⑤ quit

**B** 주어진 뜻에 알맞은 단어를 <보기>에서 찾아 쓰시오.

보기 far away nearly inside own imagine

1 to make a guess ____________
2 within the inner part ____________
3 almost but not quite ____________
4 being a long distance from a particular place ____________
5 used for showing that something belongs to a particular person ____________

## 3 Life

**A** 다음 중 단어의 정의가 잘못된 것은?

① survive: to notice or realize
② happen: to occur or take place
③ save: to rescue from harm or danger
④ advice: an opinion offered as a guide to action
⑤ basement: the part of a building that is below the level of the ground

**B** 우리말과 일치하도록 〈보기〉에서 단어를 골라 문장을 완성하시오.

보기 broken warn object protect cover

1 Look at the moving ____________ in the sky! 하늘에서 움직이는 물체를 봐!
2 Be careful of ____________ glass on the floor. 바닥에 있는 깨진 유리를 조심해라.
3 Tom tried to ____________ the children from fire. Tom은 화재로부터 아이들을 보호하려고 노력했다.
4 Use a wet towel to ____________ your mouth and nose.
당신의 입과 코를 가리는 데 젖은 수건을 이용하시오.
5 Doctors ____________ that playing computer games is bad for kids.
의사들은 컴퓨터 게임을 하는 것이 아이들에게 해롭다고 경고한다.

## 4 Opinion

**A** 밑줄 친 단어와 비슷한 의미의 단어를 고르시오.

1 He doesn't want to hurt your feelings.
① wound ② cure ③ heal ④ answer ⑤ care

2 Mom asked me to prepare dinner.
① answer ② reply ③ like ④ request ⑤ enjoy

**B** 우리말과 일치하도록 〈보기〉에서 단어를 골라 문장을 완성하시오.

보기 text once find out after all

1 ____________, every student was gathered in the hall. 결국, 모든 학생이 강당에 모였다.
2 I want to ____________ who helped me yesterday. 나는 어제 누가 나를 도와줬는지 알아내고 싶다.
3 Teens prefer to ____________ rather than make a phone call.
십 대는 전화 통화보다는 문자메시지 보내는 것을 선호한다.
4 Jason and I visit the seniors' center ____________ a week.
Jason과 나는 일주일에 한 번씩 양로원을 방문한다.

# 어휘 재충전

## 1 Food

- □ terrible a. 끔찍한, 지독한
- □ line up 줄을 서다
- □ stand n. 가판대, 좌판
- □ all over 곳곳에
- □ golden a. 노릇노릇한
- □ crispy a. 바삭한
- □ be served with ~와 함께 제공되다
- □ spicy a. 매운
- □ vinegar n. 식초
- □ sesame oil n. 참기름
- □ pickled a. (소금물이나 식초에) 절인
- □ cabbage n. 양배추
- □ cucumber n. 오이
- □ stink v. 악취를 풍기다
- □ badly ad. 몹시
- □ soak v. 적시다, 담그다
- □ broth n. 즙, 육수
- □ recipe n. 조리법
- □ hide v. 감추다, 숨다
- □ dare to 감히 ~하다

## 2 Culture

- □ vending machine n. 자동판매기
- □ invention n. 발명품, 발명
- □ nearly ad. 거의
- □ far away 멀리, 먼 곳에
- □ yummy a. 아주 맛있는
- □ soda pop 소다수
- □ look at 보다, 살펴보다
- □ even ad. 심지어
- □ lettuce n. 상추
- □ inside prep. ~의 안에
- □ imagine v. 상상하다
- □ own a. 자신의
- □ work v. 작동하다
- □ demand n. 수요

## 3 Life

- □ tornado n. 토네이도
- □ happen v. 발생하다, 일어나다
- □ turn v. (방향을) 돌리다
- □ survive v. 살아남다
- □ a bit of 약간의
- □ following a. 다음의
- □ advice n. 조언
- □ as soon as ~하자마자
- □ warning sound 경고음
- □ basement n. 지하실
- □ broken a. 깨진
- □ object n. 사물, 물체
- □ grab v. 움켜잡다
- □ pillow n. 베개
- □ cover v. 덮다
- □ hollow n. (움푹 패인) 구멍
- □ lie face down 엎드리다
- □ protect A from B B로부터 A를 보호하다
- □ save v. 구하다
- □ suck up 빨아올리다

## 4 Opinion

- □ text v. 문자메시지를 보내다
- □ ask v. 요청하다, 묻다
- □ hang out with ~와 시간을 보내다
- □ be busy -ing ~하느라 바쁘다
- □ find out 알아내다
- □ lie v. 거짓말하다
- □ nobody 누구도 ~않다
- □ even ad. 심지어, ~도
- □ make a mistake 실수하다
- □ what if ~? ~라면 어쩌지?
- □ hurt v. 다치게 하다
- □ for years 수년 동안
- □ once ad. 한 번
- □ after all 결국에는
- □ break up with ~와 절교하다
- □ work it out 해결하다

# Chapter 03

Psychology

What do you usually do when you're stressed? You might listen to music, go for a walk, or play computer games. Which works best? Well, according to a British study, it's none of the above. ① The study found that reading is the best way to relieve stress. "② Reading works better and faster than other methods such as listening to music, going for a walk, or settling down with a cup of tea. ③ It really doesn't matter what book you read. ④ Reading comic books has many negative effects on children. ⑤ By losing yourself in a book, you can escape from the worries and stress of the everyday world. Also, you can spend a moment enjoying the author's imagination," said Dr. Lewis.

**1** 윗글에서 스트레스를 푸는 가장 좋은 방법으로 언급된 것은 무엇인가?

① listening to music　② reading books
③ going for a walk　④ playing computer games
⑤ settling down with a cup of tea

**2** 윗글의 밑줄 친 ①~⑤ 중 글의 흐름과 관계가 없는 것은?

①　②　③　④　⑤ 

| | | |
|---|---|---|
| stressed a. ______ | go for a walk ______ | according to ______ |
| above n. ______ | relieve v. ______ | method n. ______ |
| settle down ______ | matter v. ______ | have an effect on ______ |
| lose yourself in A ______ | escape from ______ | moment n. ______ |
| author n. ______ | imagination n. ______ | |

A few years ago, a sixteen-year-old American student, Brianna Swinderman, collected about 2,300 pieces of luggage. Then, she gave them away as quickly as she could. Why? Brianna's mother works for the foster-care system, and Brianna saw many foster children with nothing 5 but garbage bags to carry their things in. "It sent a message that they and their possessions are trash," Brianna said. She wished the children could have proper luggage instead. She believed it would give them hope, dignity, and self-esteem. So she set up a website, presented her ideas to business leaders and civic groups, raised money, collected donations 10 of bags, and distributed them to hundreds of foster children. "Bags of Hope" was a big success and continues to grow.

*foster-care system 가정 위탁 보호 시스템

**1** Brianna Swinderman에 관한 윗글의 내용과 일치하는 것은?

① 여행을 좋아해서 2,300개의 여행용 가방을 수집했다.
② 어려서부터 가정 위탁 보호소에서 자랐다.
③ 어머니가 위탁 보호 시스템을 위해 일한다.
④ 어려운 이웃들을 위해 전 재산을 기부했다.
⑤ 위탁 아이들을 위해 '희망의 가방'을 제작하여 판매했다.

**2** 윗글에서 Brianna가 한 일로 언급된 것이 아닌 것은?

① 홈페이지 만들기 ② 모금하기 ③ 가방 기부 받기
④ 위탁 보호 시설에서 봉사하기 ⑤ 시민 단체에 아이디어 소개하기

| | | |
|---|---|---|
| collect v. ________ | give away ________ | foster a. ________ |
| nothing but ________ | garbage n. ________ | possession n. ________ |
| proper a. ________ | dignity n. ________ | self-esteem n. ________ |
| set up ________ | present v. ________ | civic a. ________ |
| raise v. ________ | donation n. ________ | distribute v. ________ |
| success n. ________ | continue v. ________ | |

3

World News

An unusual crime was reported to U.K. police last year. They found out that a whale's body parts were for sale online. The seller had 26 whale's teeth for sale at £5 each and a jawbone for £45. According to the ad, the parts came from a dead whale found on a beach in Norfolk, England. 5 The police quickly found the seller, a fourteen-year-old boy. They didn't arrest him because he was too young. But what was his crime? Rob Deauville, from London's Natural History Museum, explained. "By ancient law, whales are royal fish," he said. "Dead whales found on British beaches belong to Britain's kings and queens." Specifically, dead whales' 10 heads are the king's property, and tails are the queen's. It's because these parts were ______________________ in ancient Britain.

*jawbone 턱뼈

어휘 충전

| | | |
|---|---|---|
| unusual a. ________ | crime n. ________ | report v. ________ |
| find out ________ | whale n. ________ | for sale ________ |
| seller n. ________ | ad n. ________ | dead a. ________ |
| arrest v. ________ | ancient a. ________ | royal a. ________ |
| belong to ________ | specifically ad. ________ | property n. ________ |
| tail n. ________ | symbol n. ________ | |

**1** 윗글의 빈칸에 들어갈 말로 가장 알맞은 것은?

① symbols of U.K police
② symbols of victory
③ symbols of marine life
④ symbols of royal power
⑤ symbols of freedom

**2** 윗글에서 경찰이 판매자를 체포하지 않은 이유로 가장 알맞은 것은?

① 나이가 너무 어렸기 때문에
② 온라인에서만 판매를 했기 때문에
③ 고래를 잡는 것은 불법이 아니기 때문에
④ 영국 왕실과 관련이 있는 인물이었기 때문에
⑤ 자연사 박물관에 고래를 기증을 했기 때문에

**3** 윗글의 내용과 일치하도록 바르게 짝지어진 것은?

| | King's Property | | Queen's Property |
|---|---|---|---|
| ① | whales' tails | … | whales' heads |
| ② | whales' teeth | … | whales' heads |
| ③ | whales' jawbones | … | whales' tails |
| ④ | whales' heads | … | whales' tails |
| ⑤ | whales' heads | … | whales' teeth |

**세계의 특이한 법**

지구촌 각 나라와 주(州)에서는 실제로 적용되지만 다소 황당해 보이는 법률이 있다. 세계의 특이한 법의 사례들을 살펴보자.

❶ **프랑스** – 오전 8시부터 오후 8시 사이에 방송되는 라디오 음악 프로그램에서 70% 이상을 프랑스 작곡가들의 음악으로 방송해야만 한다.
❷ **덴마크** – 탈옥은 불법이 아니며, 탈옥 도중 체포될 경우 남은 형기만 복역하면 된다.
❸ **미국, 오클라호마 주** – 타인의 햄버거를 베어 먹는 것은 위법이다.
❹ **영국** – 영국 왕이 그려진 우표를 거꾸로 붙이는 것은 반역행위이다.
❺ **싱가포르** – 껌을 구입하려면 치과의사의 처방이 있어야 한다.

Information

What kinds of public transportation do you use? Probably buses, trains, and the subway. What else? Here are some unique forms of public transportation.

- **Cimodo** – *Gili Trawangan, Indonesia*

5 Motor vehicles aren't allowed on the tiny island of Gili Trawangan. Instead, tourists ride in cute horse-drawn carriages called *cimodo*. The carriages are brightly colored, and the horses jingle with bells.

- **Bike Taxi** – *Amsterdam, Netherlands*

Bike taxis are bikes with three wheels. They are made for three people:
10 a driver in the front and two passengers in the back. The drivers are friendly, and there's no noise, no pollution. Bike taxis are the perfect way to tour Amsterdam.

- **Gondola** – *Venice, Italy*

Gondolas used to be the main form of public transportation on Venice's
15 canals. Nowadays, they are mostly for tourists. The historic boats are paddled by standing oarsmen. They are romantic but expensive. You have to pay $135 for 40 minutes.

*oarsman 노 젓는 사람

| | | |
|---|---|---|
| public transportation ______ | probably ad. ______ | unique a. ______ |
| motor vehicle ______ | allow v. ______ | tourist n. ______ |
| horse-drawn a. ______ | carriage n. ______ | jingle v. ______ |
| wheel n. ______ | passenger n. ______ | friendly a. ______ |
| noise n. ______ | pollution n. ______ | used to ______ |
| main a. ______ | canal n. ______ | mostly ad. ______ |
| historic a. ______ | paddle v. ______ | standing a. ______ |
| romantic a. ______ | expensive a. ______ | |

**1** 윗글의 제목으로 가장 알맞은 것은?

① Various Ways to Tour Europe
② How to Use Public Transportation
③ The Fastest Form of Transportation
④ The World's Unique Forms of Transportation
⑤ Major Forms of Transportation in the Past

**2** 윗글의 내용과 일치하면 T, 그렇지 않으면 F를 쓰시오.

(1) Cimodo는 암스테르담을 관광할 수 있는 마차이다. ________
(2) Bike Taxi는 운전자를 포함하여 두 사람만 탈 수 있다. ________
(3) Gondola는 예전에는 주요 대중교통 수단이었다. ________

서술형
**3** 윗글에서 Gondola의 장점과 단점을 찾아 영어로 쓰시오.

________________________________________________

이미지 맵 글을 읽고, 빈칸을 완성하시오.

**Title**: (1)________________________________

| Cimodo | Bike Taxi | Gondola |
| --- | --- | --- |
| Gili Trawangan, Indonesia | Amsterdam, Netherlands | Venice, Italy |
| It is a horse-drawn (2)____________. | It is a bike with three (3)____________ for three people. | It is (4)____________ by a standing oarsman. |

# Review Test

## 1 Psychology

**A** 빈칸에 들어갈 알맞은 단어를 고르시오.

1 Reading is the best way to ____________ stress. 독서는 스트레스를 푸는 가장 좋은 방법이다.
① recover ② cause ③ realize ④ lose ⑤ relieve

2 You might go for a ____________ when you're stressed.
당신은 스트레스를 받을 때 산책을 갈 지도 모른다.
① play ② walk ③ talk ④ work ⑤ sing

**B** 우리말과 일치하도록 〈보기〉에서 단어를 골라 문장을 완성하시오.

보기 stressed moment imaginations above

1 That was a very dangerous ____________. 그것은 매우 위험한 순간이었다.
2 Children have creative ____________. 아이들은 창의적인 상상력을 가지고 있다.
3 You have to raise your hands ____________ your head. 너는 머리 위로 손을 들어야 한다.
4 I usually eat chocolate when I'm ____________. 나는 스트레스를 받을 때 주로 초콜릿을 먹는다.

## 2 Stories

**A** 밑줄 친 단어와 반대되는 의미의 단어를 고르시오.

1 This project will be a great success.
① fame ② fortune ③ failure ④ victory ⑤ effort

2 She tried to continue to talk with him.
① begin ② keep ③ remain ④ stay ⑤ stop

**B** 우리말과 일치하도록 〈보기〉에서 단어를 골라 문장을 완성하시오.

보기 garbage distribute present collect

1 She has to ____________ more data. 그녀는 좀 더 많은 자료를 보여줘야 한다.
2 The ____________ was picked up last night. 그 쓰레기는 어젯밤에 수거되었다.
3 He used to ____________ postcards when he was young. 그는 어렸을 때 엽서를 모으곤 했다.
4 We will ____________ free food and clothes at Christmas.
우리는 크리스마스에 무료로 음식과 옷을 나누어 줄 것이다.

정답 및 해설 p9

## 3 World News

**A** 다음 중 단어의 정의가 잘못된 것은?

① dead: no longer alive
② crime: illegal activities in general
③ royal: relating to a king or queen
④ sale: the process of selling goods
⑤ unusual: normal, common, or ordinary

**B** 우리말과 일치하도록 〈보기〉에서 단어를 골라 문장을 완성하시오.

보기 ancient symbol arrest property

1 Double-decker bus is the ____________ of London. 이층버스는 런던의 상징이다.
2 John was interested in ____________ history. John은 고대의 역사에 관심이 있었다.
3 The man will leave all his ____________ to his children. 그는 모든 재산을 자식들에게 남길 것이다.
4 They are trying every means to ____________ the criminal.
그들은 그 범인을 체포하기 위해 모든 방법을 동원하고 있다.

## Information

**A** 밑줄 친 단어와 비슷한 의미의 단어를 고르시오.

1 My mom didn't allow me to go to the party.
① give ② avoid ③ permit ④ prevent ⑤ protect

2 Her relatives seem to be friendly toward me.
① mean ② kind ③ funny ④ wild ⑤ honest

**B** 우리말과 일치하도록 〈보기〉에서 단어를 골라 문장을 완성하시오.

보기 tourists passengers pollution carriage

1 It is the biggest cause of air ____________. 그것은 대기오염의 가장 큰 원인이다.
2 Millions of ____________ visit Paris every year. 수백만 명의 관광객이 매년 파리를 방문한다.
3 There is a horse pulling the ____________ in the park. 공원에는 마차를 끄는 말 한 마리가 있다.
4 Some ____________ were slightly injured from the crash.
몇몇 승객이 충돌사고로 약간의 부상을 입었다.

## 1 Psychology

| | |
|---|---|
| □ stressed | a. 스트레스를 받는 |
| □ go for a walk | 산책하러 가다 |
| □ according to | ~에 의하면 |
| □ above | n. 위에서 말한 것 |
| □ relieve | v. 없애주다, 줄이다 |
| □ method | n. 방법 |
| □ settle down | 편안히 앉다 |
| □ matter | v. 중요하다 |
| □ have an effect on | ~에 영향을 미치다 |
| □ lose yourself in A | A에 빠지다 |
| □ escape from | ~로부터 벗어나다 |
| □ moment | n. 순간, 잠깐 |
| □ author | n. 작가 |
| □ imagination | n. 상상력 |

## 2 Stories

| | |
|---|---|
| □ collect | v. 모으다, 수집하다 |
| □ give away | (물건을) 거저 주다 |
| □ foster | a. 양~, 위탁~ |
| □ nothing but | 오직, 단지 ~뿐 |
| □ garbage | n. 쓰레기 |
| □ possession | n. 소유물, 소지품 |
| □ proper | a. 적절한, 제대로 된 |
| □ dignity | n. 자존감 |
| □ self-esteem | n. 자부심 |
| □ set up | 설립하다, 준비하다 |
| □ present | v. 보여주다, 제시하다 |
| □ civic | a. 시의, 시민의 |
| □ raise | v. (자금을) 모으다 |
| □ donation | n. 기부, 기증 |
| □ distribute | v. 나누어 주다 |
| □ success | n. 성공 |
| □ continue | v. 계속하다 |

## 3 World News

| | |
|---|---|
| □ unusual | a. 특이한, 흔치 않은 |
| □ crime | n. 범죄 |
| □ report | v. 보고하다, 알리다 |
| □ find out | 알아내다 |
| □ whale | n. 고래 |
| □ for sale | 팔려고 내놓은 |
| □ seller | n. 판매자 |
| □ ad | n. 광고 |
| □ dead | a. 죽은 |
| □ arrest | v. 체포하다 |
| □ ancient | a. 고대의 |
| □ royal | a. 국왕의 |
| □ belong to | ~의 소유이다 |
| □ specifically | ad. 구체적으로, 특히 |
| □ property | n. 재산 |
| □ tail | n. 꼬리 |
| □ symbol | n. 상징 |

## 4 Information

| | |
|---|---|
| □ public transportation | 대중교통 |
| □ probably | ad. 아마 |
| □ unique | a. 독특한, 특별한 |
| □ motor vehicle | 자동차 |
| □ allow | v. 허락하다 |
| □ tourist | n. 관광객 |
| □ horse-drawn | a. 말이 끄는 |
| □ carriage | n. 마차 |
| □ jingle | v. 딸랑거리다 |
| □ wheel | n. 바퀴 |
| □ passenger | n. 승객 |
| □ friendly | a. 친절한 |
| □ noise | n. 소음 |
| □ pollution | n. 오염, 공해 |
| □ used to | 했었다 |
| □ main | a. 주된 |
| □ canal | n. 운하, 수로 |
| □ mostly | ad. 주로 |
| □ historic | a. 역사적으로 중요한 |
| □ paddle | v. 노를 젓다 |
| □ standing | a. 서 있는 |
| □ romantic | a. 낭만적인 |
| □ expensive | a. 비싼 |

# Chapter 04

KEEP OUT
PRIVATE PROPERTY
Humor
Technology
Information
Stories

## Humor

A scholar was on a fishing trip out at sea. He was very proud of his knowledge. So, he asked the boatman, "Do you know biology?" The boatman said he did not. "Then, do you know zoology, ecology, geology, physiology…?" The boatman said no to each one. Finally the scholar said, "What on earth do you know? You'll die from your lack of education!" ______________________ the boat began to sink. The boatman shouted to the scholar, "Do you know swimminology and escapology from sharkology? "No!" the scholar shouted back. "That's too bad!" called the boatman. "Sharkology will eat your legology, handology, bodyology, and headology, and you'll die thanks to your mouthology."

**1** 윗글의 빈칸에 들어갈 말로 가장 알맞은 것은?

① Moreover ② All of a sudden ③ However
④ For example ⑤ At first

**2** 윗글의 학자를 비유한 속담으로 가장 알맞은 것은?

① 바늘 도둑이 소 도둑 된다. ② 달면 삼키고 쓰면 뱉는다.
③ 까마귀 날자 배 떨어진다. ④ 가는 말이 고와야 오는 말이 곱다.
⑤ 세 살 버릇 여든까지 간다.

| | | |
|---|---|---|
| scholar n. ________ | be proud of ________ | knowledge n. ________ |
| boatman n. ________ | biology n. ________ | zoology n. ________ |
| ecology n. ________ | geology n. ________ | physiology n. ________ |
| on earth ________ | die from ________ | lack of ________ |
| education n. ________ | sink v. ________ | shout v. ________ |
| thanks to ________ | all of a sudden ________ | |

## 2 Technology

Have you ever lost a bag at the airport? Here's a bag that's made for you! It has wheels and a folding handle and is carry-on size, just like normal carry-on bags. But it follows you ______________________. It's a robot, and it's also carry-on luggage. It's Hop! Sensors in Hop pick up signals from your cell phone. The signals track your movements and enable Hop to follow you. If Hop is held up and gets too far behind you, it locks itself and alerts your phone. Your phone tells you where Hop is, so you can easily go back and find it. Hop moves at walking speed, but its inventors are developing a faster model to keep up with travelers running to catch a flight.

*carry-on 기내에 들고 들어갈 수 있는

**1** 윗글의 빈칸에 들어갈 말로 가장 알맞은 것은?

① whatever you want ② wherever you go ③ how you feel
④ why you move ⑤ what you buy

**2** Hop에 관한 윗글의 내용과 일치하지 않는 것은?

① 바퀴가 달렸고 접히는 손잡이가 있다.
② 로봇이자 기내용 가방이다.
③ 안에 있는 센서가 휴대 전화의 신호를 받는다.
④ 주인과 거리가 멀어지면 자동으로 잠긴다.
⑤ 뛰는 속도로 움직이는 Hop이 개발되었다.

| | | |
|---|---|---|
| wheel n. ______ | folding a. ______ | handle n. ______ |
| luggage n. ______ | sensor n. ______ | signal n. ______ |
| track v. ______ | movement n. ______ | enable v. ______ |
| be held up ______ | behind prep. ______ | alert v. ______ |
| inventor n. ______ | develop v. ______ | keep up with ______ |

Information

Aromatherapy is a very popular method of healing. Pure essential oils are used to improve people's feelings of well-being. And, believe it or not, aromatherapy is also recommended for pets. Here are several good essential oils and methods for pets. First, you can mix tea tree essential oil into your dog's shampoo. This will help (free, from pests, keep, his skin). Second, you can use lavender essential oil. It smells so good that it will remove any odors from your dog. Also, lavender makes your dog calm. So if you sprinkle a few drops on your dog's bed, your sensitive dog will fall asleep easily. Lastly, you can give your dog a gentle and relaxing massage using two or three drops of olive oil. Dogs often get itchy skin, and the olive oil relieves itching.

*aromatherapy 향기 치료(아로마테라피) *essential oil (식물에서 추출한 것으로 만든) 정유
*tea tree 티트리(허브의 한 종류)

| | | |
|---|---|---|
| method n. | healing n. | pure a. |
| improve v. | well-being n. | recommend v. |
| several a. | mix v. | pest n. |
| remove v. | odor n. | calm a. |
| sprinkle v. | drop n. | sensitive a. |
| fall asleep | lastly ad. | gentle a. |
| itchy a. | relieve v. | itching n |

**1** 윗글의 주제로 가장 알맞은 것은?

① 향기 치료 시 주의할 점
② 사람들에게 행복을 느끼게 해 주는 방법
③ 애완동물과 감정 교감을 하는 방법
④ 애완동물에게 사용할 수 있는 향기 치료
⑤ 애완동물에게 향기 치료를 사용해야 하는 이유

**2** 윗글에서 예민한 애완동물을 차분하게 만들 수 있는 방법으로 언급된 것은?

① 티트리 오일로 씻겨 줘라.
② 올리브 오일로 마사지를 해 줘라.
③ 영양가를 고려하여 먹이를 줘라.
④ 빗으로 털을 자주 빗겨 줘라.
⑤ 라벤더 오일을 몇 방울 뿌려 줘라.

**3** 윗글의 ( ) 안에 주어진 단어를 바르게 배열하여 문장을 완성하시오.

________________________________________

**아로마테라피(Aromatherapy)**

아로마테라피(aromatherapy)는 아로마(aroma: 향기, 방향)와 테라피(therapy: 치료, 요법)를 합성한 용어이다. 이는 식물에서 추출한 순수 오일의 향기를 이용해 심신을 치유하는 치료법이다.
아로마테라피는 고대 이집트에서부터 사용되었으며, 문헌에 따르면 고대 이집트인들은 미라의 방부 처리, 종교의식, 여인들이 사용하는 화장수 등에 향을 사용했다고 한다. 중세를 거쳐 약제사들에 의해 향기를 이용한 치료법이 시행되었고, 중국과 인도에서도 향을 사용했다는 기록이 있다. 현대에는 식물에서 추출한 다양한 오일을 식품, 미용, 제약 부분에서 여러 가지 형태로 이용하고 있다.

4

Stories

KEEP OUT
PRIVATE PROPERTY

Police in a town in far north Queensland, Australia, responded to an emergency call. "There's a huge crocodile outside a house!" the caller said. ( ① ) So two police officers jumped into their car and drove there as fast as they could. ( ② ) They saw the crocodile under some mango trees in the front yard of the house. ( ③ ) Immediately, a man came running out of the house. ( ④ ) "Don't shoot!" He shouted. "That's my masterpiece! It doesn't bite, it can't walk or run, and it will never eat anyone." ( ⑤ ) So, carefully, the officers walked over to take a close look. The crocodile didn't move. They gave it a little kick. It was as hard as a rock. "Naughty kids are always stealing mangoes from my garden," said the man. "This works better than a fence and a KEEP OUT sign."

| | | |
|---|---|---|
| respond to ________ | emergency n. ________ | huge a. ________ |
| crocodile n. ________ | jump into ________ | front yard ________ |
| immediately ad. ________ | come running ________ | shoot v. ________ |
| masterpiece n. ________ | bite v. ________ | carefully ad. ________ |
| take a close look ________ | naughty a. ________ | steal v. ________ |
| fence n. ________ | Keep Out ________ | take out ________ |
| gun n. ________ | prepare v. ________ | |

**1** 글의 흐름으로 보아 주어진 문장이 들어갈 위치로 가장 알맞은 곳은?

They took out their guns and prepared to shoot.

① ② ③ ④ ⑤

**2** 윗글의 내용과 일치하면 T, 그렇지 않으면 F를 쓰시오.

(1) 두 명의 경찰관이 악어의 존재를 확인하기 위해 출동했다. ________

(2) 집 앞마당에 있는 악어는 다쳐서 움직일 수 없다. ________

(3) 아이들이 정원에 있는 망고를 훔쳐간다. ________

서술형

**3** 윗글에서 앞마당의 악어가 하는 역할을 찾아 네 단어의 영어로 쓰시오.

________________________________________

이미지 맵 글을 읽고, 빈칸을 완성하시오.

**Title**: A Crocodile in the Garden

Two police officers were sent to respond to an (1)___________ call.

→ There was a crocodile in the garden, and the officers (2)___________ to shoot.

↓ Suddenly, a man came (3)___________ out of the house. Then, he said it wasn't a real one.

← He put it there because the crocodile is (4)___________ than a fence and a KEEP OUT sign.

# Review Test

## 1 Humor

**A 빈칸에 들어갈 알맞은 단어를 고르시오.**

1 He was very ______________ of his knowledge. 그는 자기의 지식이 자랑스러웠다.
① cool ② proud ③ terrible ④ famous ⑤ known

2 You'll die ______________ your lack of education! 당신은 교육 부족으로 죽게 될 거예요!
① in ② of ③ from ④ to ⑤ at

**B 우리말과 일치하도록 〈보기〉에서 단어를 골라 문장을 완성하시오.**

보기 geology scholar thanks to sink

1 Mr. Ken is both a ____________ and politician. Ken 씨는 학자이자 정치가이다.

2 I could finish the work ____________ your help. 네 도움 덕분에 내가 그 일을 마칠 수 있었다.

3 The huge rock will ____________ to the bottom of the river.
그 큰 바위는 강 바닥으로 가라앉을 것이다.

4 He's going to take a ____________ course this semester.
그는 이번 학기에 지질학 강좌를 수강할 예정이다.

## 2 Technology

**A 밑줄 친 단어와 반대되는 의미의 단어를 고르시오.**

1 This new bike enables you to move anywhere.
① permit ② allow ③ approve ④ let ⑤ prevent

2 The museum is behind the post office.
① next ② rear ③ front ④ after ⑤ back

**B 우리말과 일치하도록 〈보기〉에서 단어를 골라 문장을 완성하시오.**

보기 signals folding keep up track

1 Go and bring a ____________ chair to the garden. 가서 접히는 의자를 정원으로 가져와라.

2 He was so fast that I couldn't ____________ with him.
그가 너무 빨라서 나는 그를 따라잡을 수 없었다.

3 The detective walked quickly to ____________ the suspect.
형사는 용의자를 추적하기 위해 빠르게 걸었다.

4 Some people think aliens may send ____________ to the Earth.
몇몇 사람들은 외계인들이 지구로 신호를 보낼 지도 모른다고 생각한다.

정답 및 해설 p12

## 3 Information

**A** 〈보기〉의 밑줄 친 drop과 같은 의미로 쓰인 것은?

보기 Sprinkle a drop of lavender oil on your dog's bed.

① The temperature has dropped.
② Put the chicken on the plate and add a few drops of lemon.
③ Be careful not to drop the vase.
④ Can you drop me off in front of the library?
⑤ She dropped her bag with surprise.

**B** 우리말과 일치하도록 〈보기〉에서 단어를 골라 문장을 완성하시오.

보기 method sensitive odor itchy

1 Sometimes, I feel ____________ on my legs. 가끔 나는 다리가 가렵다.
2 What is this unpleasant ____________ in the house? 집에서 나는 이 불쾌한 냄새는 뭐야?
3 He is very ____________ about his bright red hair. 그는 자신의 밝은 빨강머리에 대해 매우 민감하다.
4 We're discussing which ____________ is needed to solve this trouble.
우리는 이 문제를 해결하기 위해 어떤 방법이 필요한지 논의 중이다.

## 4 Stories

**A** 밑줄 친 단어와 비슷한 의미의 단어를 고르시오.

1 Do I have to respond to this matter now?
① ask ② question ③ leave ④ answer ⑤ reject

2 Nathan prepared special food to serve the guests.
① arrange ② forget ③ stop ④ refuse ⑤ ignore

**B** 우리말과 일치하도록 〈보기〉에서 단어를 골라 문장을 완성하시오.

보기 took out immediately masterpiece naughty

1 I think the old picture is a(n) ____________. 내 생각에 그 오래된 그림은 걸작이다.
2 A(n) ____________ boy rang the bell and ran away. 한 장난꾸러기 소년이 벨을 누르고 도망갔다.
3 I ____________ my new cell phone from my pocket. 나는 주머니에서 새 휴대 전화를 꺼냈다.
4 When he heard a strange noise, he called 911 ____________.
그는 수상한 소리를 듣고, 즉시 911에 전화를 걸었다.

# 어휘 재충전

## 1 Humor

|  |  |
|---|---|
| □ scholar | n. 학자 |
| □ be proud of | ~을 자랑스러워하다 |
| □ knowledge | n. 지식 |
| □ boatman | n. 뱃사공 |
| □ biology | n. 생물학 |
| □ zoology | n. 동물학 |
| □ ecology | n. 생태학 |
| □ geology | n. 지질학 |
| □ physiology | n. 생리학 |
| □ on earth | 도대체, 대체 |
| □ die from | ~으로 죽다 |
| □ lack of | ~이 부족한 |
| □ education | n. 교육 |
| □ sink | v. 가라앉다 |
| □ shout | v. 소리치다 |
| □ thanks to | ~덕분에 |
| □ all of a sudden | 갑자기 |

## 2 Technology

|  |  |
|---|---|
| □ wheel | n. 바퀴 |
| □ folding | a. 접을 수 있는 |
| □ handle | n. 손잡이 |
| □ luggage | n. 짐, 수하물 |
| □ sensor | n. 센서, 감지기 |
| □ signal | n. 신호 |
| □ track | v. 추적하다, 뒤쫓다 |
| □ movement | n. 움직임 |
| □ enable | v. ~할 수 있게 하다 |
| □ be held up | 방해받다, 늦추어지다 |
| □ behind | prep. 뒤에 |
| □ alert | v. 위험을 알리다 |
| □ inventor | n. 발명가 |
| □ develop | v. 개발하다 |
| □ keep up with | ~을 따라잡다, 뒤지지 않다 |

## 3 Information

|  |  |
|---|---|
| □ method | n. 방법 |
| □ healing | n. 치유, 치료 |
| □ pure | a. 다른 것이 섞이지 않은 |
| □ improve | v. 개선하다, 증진하다 |
| □ well-being | n. 안녕, 행복, 복지 |
| □ recommend | v. 추천하다 |
| □ several | a. (몇)몇의 |
| □ mix | v. 섞다 |
| □ pest | n. 해충 |
| □ remove | v. 제거하다 |
| □ odor | n. 냄새, 악취 |
| □ calm | a. 침착한, 차분한 |
| □ sprinkle | v. 뿌리다 |
| □ drop | n. 방울 |
| □ sensitive | a. 예민한, 민감한 |
| □ fall asleep | 잠들다 |
| □ lastly | ad. 마지막으로 |
| □ gentle | a. 부드러운 |
| □ itchy | a. 가려운 |
| □ relieve | v. 없애주다, 덜어주다 |
| □ itching | n. 가려움 |

## 4 Stories

|  |  |
|---|---|
| □ respond to | ~에 응답하다 |
| □ emergency | n. 비상, 긴급 |
| □ huge | a. 거대한 |
| □ crocodile | n. 악어 |
| □ jump into | 뛰어 올라타다 |
| □ front yard | 앞뜰, 앞마당 |
| □ immediately | ad. 즉시 |
| □ come running | 한달음에 달려오다 |
| □ shoot | v. 쏘다 |
| □ masterpiece | n. 걸작, 명작 |
| □ bite | v. 물다 |
| □ carefully | ad. 조심스럽게 |
| □ take a close look | 주의 깊게 살펴보다 |
| □ naughty | a. 버릇없는, 말썽꾸러기의 |
| □ steal | v. 훔치다 |
| □ fence | n. 울타리 |
| □ Keep Out | 출입금지 |
| □ take out | 꺼내다 |
| □ gun | n. 총 |
| □ prepare | v. 준비하다 |

# Chapter 05

Body

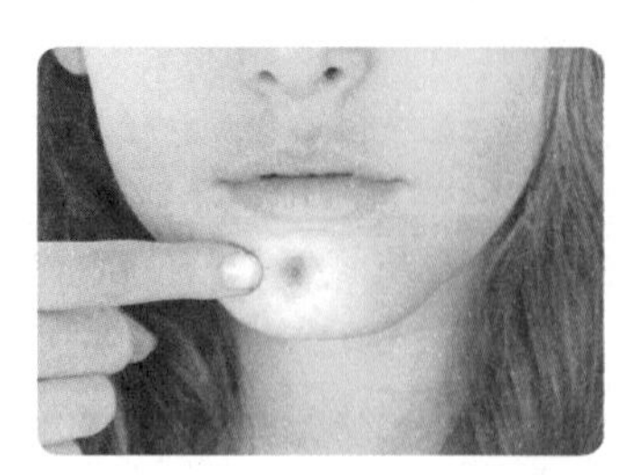

Acne can be a big problem for teenagers. ( ① ) Teenage hormones are very active and can make the skin too oily. ( ② ) But acne can be kept under control. ( ③ ) First, wash your face morning and night with a mild cleanser. ( ④ ) Washing too much with harsh soaps only hurts your skin and makes acne worse. ( ⑤ ) That's because when your skin is too dry, it produces more oil. Second, don't touch, squeeze, or pick at spots. Doing this spreads infections, delays healing, and causes scarring. Third, avoid fatty foods and sugar. They just make more oil. Finally, if your acne is serious, see a professional skin doctor. He will give you proper treatment.

**1** 윗글에서 피부과 의사의 조언으로 언급된 것이 아닌 것은?

① Wash as often as possible with soap.
② Don't touch spots.
③ Don't eat fatty food.
④ Wash your face with a mild cleanser.
⑤ Go to see a professional skin doctor.

**2** 글의 흐름으로 보아 주어진 문장이 들어갈 위치로 가장 적절한 곳은?

> Here's some general advice from skin doctors.

① ② ③ ④ ⑤

어휘 충전

| | | |
|---|---|---|
| acne n. ______ | teenage a. ______ | hormone n. ______ |
| active a. ______ | oily a. ______ | keep under control ______ |
| mild a. ______ | cleanser n. ______ | harsh a. ______ |
| produce v. ______ | squeeze v. ______ | pick at ______ |
| spot n. ______ | spread v. ______ | infection n. ______ |
| delay v. ______ | cause v. ______ | scar v. ______ |
| avoid v. ______ | professional a. ______ | proper a. ______ |
| treatment n. ______ | | |

Culture

West Aceh province in Indonesia is strictly Muslim. Recently the provincial government made a new law. The law says that Muslim women cannot wear pants that fit too tightly. "It is against Islamic teaching for women to show their curves," said a government official. So, Aceh police officers carry long skirts when they are on duty, and they look at every woman on the streets very carefully. If a woman is dressed in skinny pants, the police stop her. They give her a long skirt to put on and take her to the police station. There, she has to listen to a lesson from a Muslim preacher. The purpose of this is to remind her that pure Muslim women in Aceh should never wear tight pants.

*Muslim 이슬람교의, 이슬람교

**1** 윗글에서 밑줄 친 new law의 내용으로 가장 알맞은 것은?

① 이슬람 여성은 짧은 치마를 입을 수 없다.
② 이슬람 여성은 딱 붙는 바지를 입을 수 없다.
③ 이슬람 여성은 전도사로부터 교육을 받아야 한다.
④ 이슬람 여성은 혼자서 길거리를 걸어 다닐 수 없다.
⑤ 이슬람 여성은 낯선 남자와 이야기를 나눌 수 없다.

서술형

**2** 윗글의 밑줄 친 this가 의미하는 것을 찾아 우리말로 쓰시오.

_______________________________________________

| | | |
|---|---|---|
| province n. ______ | strictly ad. ______ | provincial a. ______ |
| government n. ______ | fit v. ______ | tightly ad. ______ |
| against prep. ______ | Islamic a. ______ | curve n. ______ |
| official n. ______ | on duty ______ | skinny a. ______ |
| put on ______ | preacher n. ______ | purpose n. ______ |
| remind v. ______ | pure a. ______ | |

Information

In classrooms all over the world, chewing gum is not allowed. Mainly this is because chewing gum in front of elders is considered to be rude. It's also because students stick chewed-up gum under desks and chairs. 5 ________________, many teachers believe it disturbs students' concentration. But in a recent study, chewing gum seemed to help students get better scores in math. The study involved 108 students, aged from 13 to 16, and was carried out for 14 weeks. Half of the students chewed gum during math class, and the other half did not. During the 10 14 weeks, the students who chewed gum raised their math test scores by 3 percent. The other students' scores remained steady. According to the head researcher, it's a small but meaningful result. "It suggests that chewing gum has a positive effect on concentration," she said.

| | | |
|---|---|---|
| chew v. ________ | allow v. ________ | mainly ad. ________ |
| elder n. ________ | consider v. ________ | rude a. ________ |
| stick v. ________ | chew up ________ | disturb v. ________ |
| concentration n. ________ | involve v. ________ | aged from A to B ________ |
| carry out ________ | raise v. ________ | remain v. ________ |
| steady a. ________ | head n. ________ | meaningful a. ________ |
| result n. ________ | suggest v. ________ | positive a. ________ |
| have an effect on ________ | | |

**1** 윗글의 주제로 가장 알맞은 것은?

① how to get high scores in math
② a positive effect of chewing gum
③ a new type of chewing gum for students
④ chewing gum that disturbs your concentration
⑤ reasons why chewing gum is not allowed in classrooms

**2** 윗글의 빈칸에 들어갈 말로 가장 알맞은 것은?

① For example ② Nevertheless ③ Furthermore
④ However ⑤ On the other hand

**3** 밑줄 친 recent study에 관한 윗글의 내용과 일치하지 않는 것은?

① 108명의 학생이 참여했다.
② 14주 동안 진행되었다.
③ 참여한 학생의 3%는 수학 점수가 올랐다.
④ 껌을 씹지 않은 학생들의 점수는 변화가 없었다.
⑤ 참여한 학생을 반으로 나누어 조사를 했다.

**껌과 관련된 다양한 연구 결과**

- 미국 세인트로렌스 대학 심리학과 서지 오나이퍼 교수의 연구 결과에 따르면 시험 직전 5분간 껌을 씹으면 껌을 씹지 않은 학생들보다 시험 점수가 높게 나온다. 이는 시험을 시작한 후 20분 동안 지속하는 것으로 나타났다. 껌을 씹는 동안 턱관절 운동이 뇌를 활성화시켜 집중력을 높여 줄 뿐만 아니라 각성 효과를 불러온다는 것이다.
- 영국의 카디프대 연구진은 껌을 씹으면서 과제를 외우면 암기력이 훨씬 높고 정확했다는 연구 결과를 내놓았다.
- 미국의 치아 연구저널은 역류성 식도염을 앓고 있으면 껌을 씹는 것이 산성도를 정상으로 돌아오게 하여 증상을 완화해준다는 결과를 내놓았다.
- 껌은 입 냄새뿐만 아니라 플라크 제거에도 효과적이다. 일부 껌에 들어있는 자일리톨 성분은 타액의 분비를 촉진해 소화를 도와주고, 부식을 일으키는 무탄스균의 서식을 방지해 충치 예방에 도움을 준다.

# 4

Origin

In England in the 18th and 19th centuries, boar hunting was a popular sport. Noblemen carried guns and walked through the woods to hunt wild boars. Meanwhile, the noblemen's servants walked ahead and beat on branches. The beating noise scared boars. It made them run out from the thick bushes where they lived. Then, the hunters tried to shoot them. But boars are very dangerous and can easily kill a man. Since the servants did not have guns, they did not go into the bushes. Instead, they beat "around" them. By "beating around the bush," they tried to avoid harm. Today, "beating around the bush" still means trying to avoid trouble. People try to avoid trouble by not saying exactly what they mean. So, when someone says, "stop beating around the bush," it means "hurry up and get to the point."

*boar 멧돼지, 수퇘지

**1** 윗글의 제목으로 가장 알맞은 것은?

① How to Survive in the Woods
② Why the Servants Didn't Have Guns
③ The Purpose of Beating on Branches
④ A Method of Hunting Wild Boars in the Bushes
⑤ The Origin of the Expression "Beating around the Bush"

| | | |
|---|---|---|
| nobleman n. ______ | through prep. ______ | woods n. ______ |
| hunt v. ______ | meanwhile ad. ______ | servant n. ______ |
| beat on ______ | scare v. ______ | run out ______ |
| bush n. ______ | dangerous a. ______ | go into ______ |
| avoid v. ______ | harm n. ______ | exactly ad. ______ |
| get to the point ______ | | |

**2** 하인들이 숲 안으로 들어가지 않고 숲 주변에 있던 이유는 무엇인가?

① 하인들은 총이 없었기 때문에
② 사냥에 관심이 없었기 때문에
③ 새로운 사냥감을 찾아야 했기 때문에
④ 귀족들만 숲 안으로 들어갈 수 있기 때문에
⑤ 수퇘지가 숲 밖으로 나오는 것을 막기 위해

**3** 오늘날 beating around the bush가 쓰이는 의미로 가장 알맞은 것은?

① 요점을 정확하게 말하다.
② 말을 빙빙 돌리다.
③ 너무 빠르게 이야기하다.
④ 상대방을 이야기를 주의 깊게 듣다.
⑤ 거침없이 이야기하다.

이미지 맵 글을 읽고, 빈칸을 완성하시오.

**Title**:
(1)______________
______________
______________

In England, (2)______________ was a popular sport and noblemen went into the bushes to hunt wild boars.

Their (3)______________ beat around the bushes instead of going into them.

The (4)______________ noise made the boars run out of the bushes and helped the servants avoid harm.

Today, it still means trying to avoid (5)______________.

# Review Test

## 1 Body

**A 빈칸에 알맞은 단어를 고르시오.**

1 Acne can be kept under ____________. 여드름을 억제할 수 있다.
① cover ② control ③ age ④ contact ⑤ way

2 The skin doctors will give you proper ____________.
피부과 의사가 당신에게 적절한 치료법을 제시해 줄 것이다.
① technology ② promise ③ treatment ④ explanation ⑤ advice

**B 우리말과 일치하도록 〈보기〉에서 단어를 골라 문장을 완성하시오.**

보기 oily delay scar squeeze

1 She has a burn ____________ on her left hand. 그녀는 왼손에 화상 자국이 있다.
2 I'm looking for a product for ____________ skin. 나는 지성 피부를 위한 제품을 찾고 있다.
3 I always ____________ the toothpaste from the end. 나는 항상 치약을 끝에서부터 짜서 쓴다.
4 We wanted to ____________ the meeting for an hour. 우리는 회의를 1시간 뒤로 미루고 싶었다.

## 2 Culture

**A 밑줄 친 단어와 반대되는 의미의 단어를 고르시오.**

1 She put on a pink dress and went to the party.
① take out ② get on ③ pick up ④ put off ⑤ take off

2 The nurse bandaged my arm tightly.
① loosely ② strictly ③ slightly ④ particularly ⑤ rapidly

**B 우리말과 일치하도록 〈보기〉에서 단어를 골라 문장을 완성하시오.**

보기 remind fit against purpose

1 Most of the students are ____________ the new rules. 학생 대부분은 새로운 규칙에 반대했다.
2 The skirt is fine, but the blouse doesn't ____________. 치마는 좋았지만, 블라우스는 맞지 않았다.
3 I'm not sure about the main ____________ of this contest. 나는 이 대회의 주요 목적을 잘 모르겠다.
4 Jenny called to ____________ me of my homework.
Jenny는 나에게 숙제를 상기시켜 주려고 전화했다.

정답 및 해설 p15

## 3 Information

### A 〈보기〉의 밑줄 친 raised와 같은 의미로 쓰인 것은?

보기 The students who chewed gum raised their math test scores by 3 percent.

① My grandpa raised tomatoes.
② She has raised two daughters alone.
③ Slowly raise your upper body.
④ The sellers raise the price every year.
⑤ They raised money for charity.

### B 우리말과 일치하도록 〈보기〉에서 단어를 골라 문장을 완성하시오.

보기 concentration positive rude stick

1 I didn't ____________ a stamp on the envelope. 나는 봉투에 우표를 붙이지 않았다.
2 He couldn't stand their ____________ words. 그는 그들의 무례한 말을 참을 수 없었다.
3 It's important to have a ____________ attitude. 긍정적인 태도를 지니는 것은 중요하다.
4 This music will improve your ____________. 이 음악은 너의 집중력을 향상시켜 줄 것이다.

## 4 Origin

### A 밑줄 친 단어와 비슷한 의미의 단어를 고르시오.

1 He warned me that the machine was dangerous.
① excited ② careful ③ dirty ④ safe ⑤ risky

2 People wear sunscreen to avoid skin damage from the sun.
① provide ② prevent ③ improve ④ allow ⑤ respect

### B 우리말과 일치하도록 〈보기〉에서 단어를 골라 문장을 완성하시오.

보기 harm beating went into shoot

1 Did he ____________ the bird in the forest? 그가 숲에서 새를 쏘았니?
2 A lot of people ____________ the stadium. 많은 사람들이 운동장으로 들어갔다.
3 He could hear his heart ____________ in his chest. 그는 가슴에서 심장이 뛰는 소리를 들을 수 있었다.
4 He meant no ____________, but I was disappointed in him.
그가 해를 끼치려 한 것은 아니지만, 나는 그에게 실망했다.

# 어휘 재충전

## 1 Body

- □ acne n. 여드름
- □ teenage a. 십 대의
- □ hormone n. 호르몬
- □ active a. 활발한
- □ oily a. 지성의, 유분이 많은
- □ keep under control 억제하다
- □ mild a. 순한
- □ cleanser n. 세안제
- □ harsh a. 너무 강한, 가혹한
- □ produce v. 만들어 내다
- □ squeeze v. 짜다
- □ pick at ~을 만지작거리다
- □ spot n. 발진, 뾰루지
- □ spread v. 퍼뜨리다, 펼치다
- □ infection n. 감염, 전염병
- □ delay v. 지연시키다
- □ cause v. ~의 원인이 되다
- □ scar v. 상처 자국이 남다
- □ avoid v. 방지하다, 피하다
- □ professional a. 전문적인
- □ proper a. 적절한
- □ treatment n. 치료, 처치

## 2 Culture

- □ province n. 지방, 주
- □ strictly ad. 엄격히
- □ provincial a. 지방의, 주의
- □ government n. 정부, 정권
- □ fit v. 맞다, 적합하다
- □ tightly ad. 꽉, 단단히
- □ against prep. ~에 반대하여
- □ Islamic a. 이슬람교의
- □ curve n. 곡선, (여성의) 곡선미
- □ official n. 공무원, 관리원
- □ on duty 근무 중인
- □ skinny a. 몸에 딱 맞는
- □ put on 입다
- □ preacher n. 설교사, 전도사
- □ purpose n. 목적
- □ remind v. 상기시키다
- □ pure a. 순수한

## 3 Information

- □ chew v. 씹다
- □ allow v. 허락하다
- □ mainly ad. 주로, 대부분
- □ elder n. 연장자
- □ consider v. 여기다, 생각하다
- □ rude a. 무례한, 예의 없는
- □ stick v. 붙이다
- □ chew up 씹다
- □ disturb v. 방해하다
- □ concentration n. 집중
- □ involve v. 참여시키다
- □ aged from A to B A부터 B까지 나이인
- □ carry out 수행하다
- □ raise v. 올리다
- □ remain v. 계속 ~이다
- □ steady a. 변함없는
- □ head n. 수석, 장
- □ meaningful a. 의미 있는
- □ result n. 결과
- □ suggest v. 시사하다, 제안하다
- □ positive a. 긍정적인
- □ have an effect on ~에 영향을 미치다

## 4 Origin

- □ nobleman n. 귀족
- □ through prep. ~을 관통하여
- □ woods n. 수풀, 산림
- □ hunt v. 사냥하다
- □ meanwhile ad. 그동안에
- □ servant n. 하인, 종
- □ beat on 두드리다
- □ scare v. 겁주다
- □ run out 뛰쳐나가다
- □ bush n. 관목, 덤불
- □ dangerous a. 위험한
- □ go into ~에 들어가다
- □ avoid v. 방지하다, 막다
- □ harm n. 해, 피해
- □ exactly ad. 정확히
- □ get to the point 요점을 언급하다

# Chapter 06

Letters

Dear Amanda,

Hey! How are you?

I had an amazing dream about Kelly last night. She's the classmate I told you about, remember? I told you I don't like her. And I said I could never get along with her. To me, she seemed a bit mean and stubborn. So I often got into arguments with her. But in my dream, we were friends! She was lovely. She smiled at me, and (made / her smile / me / so good / feel). We talked so easily, and we had lots in common. So, this morning I smiled at her and said hello. Then she smiled brightly back at me! We ate and hung out together at lunch. Just like in my dream, we talked easily and had a lot in common! I can't wait to see her again! What an amazing dream it was! Talk soon!

Love,

*Cindy*

**1** 윗글에서 내가 친구 Kelly에게 갖게 된 감정으로 가장 알맞은 것은?

① jealousy ② hate ③ friendship ④ pity ⑤ anger

**2** 윗글의 ( ) 안에 주어진 단어를 바르게 배열하여 문장을 완성하시오.

______________________________

amazing a. ________
seem v. ________
stubborn a. ________
have in common ________
jealousy n. ________
classmate n. ________
a bit ________
get into ________
brightly ad. ________
pity n. ________
get along with ________
mean a. ________
argument n. ________
hang out ________

Psychology

People often think, "If I never do anything wrong, then others will like me more." But they should think again. The fact is that people who make mistakes are more likable. Messing up is human. It draws others towards us more. The results of interesting tests support this theory. In one 5 test, students listened to recordings of quiz contestants. In some of the recordings, a contestant knocked over a glass of water. Later, the listeners were asked to give each contestant a score for ________________. And who got the highest score? The contestant who spilled the glass of water. It's really OK to make little mistakes now and then. In fact, 10 it's better than trying to be perfect.

**1** 윗글의 빈칸에 들어갈 말로 가장 알맞은 것은?

① wealth ② likability ③ responsibility
④ ability ⑤ politeness

서술형
**2** 윗글에서 알맞은 말을 찾아 다음 요약문을 완성하시오.

The test shows that people who make __________ are more likable.
You don't need to try to be __________.

| | | |
|---|---|---|
| make a mistake ________ | likable a. ________ | mess up ________ |
| draw v. ________ | support v. ________ | theory n. ________ |
| recording n. ________ | contestant n. ________ | knock over ________ |
| spill n. ________ | now and then ________ | perfect a. ________ |
| likability n. ________ | responsibility n. ________ | ability n. ________ |
| politeness n. ________ | | |

## Science

Did you know that the poop of giant pandas could help fight global warming? Researchers studied giant pandas' diets and discovered something very special in their poop. An adult panda can eat 10-20 kg of bamboo trees every day. The bamboo trees change very quickly into sugar in the panda's stomach. The sugar gives the panda all the energy it needs. How does the panda turn bamboo into sugar so well? It's because of the special stuff in its stomach. A little bit of it comes out in the panda's poop. If we made the special stuff in a lab, we could make lots of energy from bamboo. We could use bamboo instead of fossil fuels. That would reduce greenhouse gases. Panda poop power could make a brighter future!

| | | |
|---|---|---|
| poop n. ______ | global warming ______ | diet n. ______ |
| discover v. ______ | bamboo tree n. ______ | change into ______ |
| sugar n. ______ | stomach n. ______ | turn A into B ______ |
| stuff n. ______ | a little bit of ______ | come out ______ |
| lab n. ______ | lots of ______ | instead of ______ |
| fossil fuel ______ | reduce v. ______ | endangered a. ______ |

**1** 윗글의 제목으로 가장 알맞은 것은?

① What Giant Pandas Eat

② The Effect of Bamboo Trees

③ The Panda: An Endangered Animal

④ The Useful Material in Pandas' Poop

⑤ How Bamboo Trees Turn into Sugar

**2** 윗글의 내용과 일치하면 T, 그렇지 않으면 F를 쓰시오.

(1) 당은 판다가 필요로 하는 모든 에너지를 제공한다. ________

(2) 다 자란 판다는 일주일에 10에서 20킬로그램의 대나무를 먹는다. ________

(3) 판다의 배설물에 특별한 뭔가가 있다는 것이 발견되었다. ________

**3** 윗글에서 밑줄 친 the special stuff가 하는 일을 찾아 우리말로 쓰시오.

______________________________________________

**바다의 로또, 용연향**

영국의 Ken Wilman은 자신의 애완견 덕분에 큰 돈을 벌었다. 그가 바닷가를 산책하고 있을 때, 그의 애완견이 '바다의 로또'라고도 알려진 용연향을 발견한 것이다. 용연향이란 수컷 향유고래의 배설물이다. 일반적으로 사람들은 배설물을 더럽고 불필요한 존재라고 여기지만, 이 용연향은 향수를 만들 때 꼭 필요한 재료가 될 뿐만 아니라, 세계 3대 향 중 하나이다. Ken Wilman은 처음에 용연향의 냄새가 너무 끔찍해서 그냥 버렸지만 자신이 본 것이 무엇인지 궁금했던 그는 집에서 인터넷으로 검색해 본 후, 깜짝 놀랐다고 한다. 그가 발견한 것이 바로 용연향이었고 한화로 약 2억 700만원 가치였다.

## Opinion

You might blame science fiction. People think it will be possible to live on another planet one day. Would you like to? Let's see what Sandra and Ivan say about it.

**Sandra**: I never want to leave Earth. I think it must be 5 the most beautiful planet in the universe. ___(A)___, Earth needs us to stay here and take care of it. ① People have made a mess of lots of things on Earth. ② We can't just leave. ③ We need to clean up our mess and make the world a better place.

**Ivan**: ④ This planet is already too crowded and polluted. ⑤ That's why 10 we have to read science fiction more and more. I want to live somewhere that's cleaner and quieter. People need more space! ___(B)___, there are too many natural disasters, and they keep getting worse. So I think Earth is kind of dangerous. I want to live in a safer world. A planet without big floods, fires, or storms would be really great.

| | | |
|---|---|---|
| blame v. ______ | science fiction ______ | possible a. ______ |
| planet n. ______ | the universe ______ | take care of ______ |
| make a mess of ______ | clean up ______ | mess n. ______ |
| crowded a. ______ | polluted a. ______ | space n. ______ |
| natural disaster ______ | get worse ______ | kind of ______ |
| flood n. ______ | besides ______ | nevertheless ad. ______ |

**1** 윗글의 빈칸 (A)와 (B)에 들어갈 말이 바르게 짝지어진 것은?

① Then – Therefore
② For example – However
③ Besides – Nevertheless
④ Besides – In addition
⑤ Then – In other words

**2** 윗글을 읽고, Sandra와 Ivan의 의견으로 알맞은 것을 <보기>에서 골라 그 기호를 쓰시오.

보기
ⓐ 우리는 지구를 좀 더 나은 장소로 만들 필요가 있다.
ⓑ 지구는 너무 복잡하고 오염됐다.
ⓒ 지구는 우주에서 가장 아름다운 행성임이 틀림없다.
ⓓ 홍수나 화재가 없는 행성이 좋을 것 같다.

(A) Sandra: ______________ (B) Ivan: ______________

**3** 윗글의 밑줄 친 ①~⑤ 중 글의 흐름과 관계가 없는 것은?

① ② ③ ④ ⑤

이미지 맵 글을 읽고, 빈칸을 완성하시오.

**Title**: Do You Want to Move to Another Planet?

| Sandra | Ivan |
| --- | --- |
| Earth is the most beautiful planet in the (1)______________. | Earth is already too crowded and (3)______________. |
| People need to (2)______________ their mess and make Earth a better place. | There are too many natural disasters, and they keep getting (4)______________. |
| | Earth is kind of dangerous. We need a (5)______________ place. |

# Review Test

## 1 Letters

**A 빈칸에 들어갈 알맞은 단어를 고르시오.**

1 Mike and I have a lot ____________. Mike와 나는 공통점이 많다.
① in common ② by chance ③ of differences ④ of difficulties ⑤ of experience

2 Do you get along ____________ your new classmates? 너는 새로 온 학생과 잘 지내니?
① from ② in ③ on ④ with ⑤ for

**B 우리말과 일치하도록 〈보기〉에서 단어를 골라 문장을 완성하시오.**

보기 mean stubborn argument hung out

1 Jenny often ____________ at the beach. Jenny는 종종 해변에서 시간을 보냈다.

2 At the end of an ____________, the problem was settled. 논쟁 끝에 그 문제가 해결됐다.

3 The man is so ____________ that I can't trust him.
그 남자가 너무 짓궂어서 나는 그를 믿을 수 없다.

4 My uncle never listens to anyone. He is so ____________.
우리 삼촌은 어떤 사람의 말도 듣지 않는다. 그는 아주 고집불통이다.

## 2 Psychology

**A 밑줄 친 단어와 반대되는 의미의 단어를 고르시오.**

1 Nathan is a very likable person to me.
① attractive ② unpleasant ③ charming ④ appealing ⑤ friendly

2 Today is perfect for doing the laundry.
① excellent ② supreme ③ ideal ④ great ⑤ incomplete

**B 우리말과 일치하도록 〈보기〉에서 단어를 골라 문장을 완성하시오.**

보기 support messes up spilled theory

1 Look here, he always ____________ his room. 이것 봐, 그는 항상 자기 방을 엉망으로 만들어.

2 The little boy ____________ milk on my new shirt. 그 작은 소년이 나의 새 셔츠에 우유를 쏟았다.

3 This ____________ is focusing on the practical technique.
이 이론은 실용적인 기술에 초점을 맞추고 있다.

4 Dave has worked day and night to ____________ his family.
Dave는 가족을 부양하기 위해 밤낮으로 일해왔다.

정답 및 해설 p18

## 3 Science

**A** 〈보기〉의 밑줄 친 change와 다른 의미로 쓰인 것은?

보기 The bamboo trees change very quickly into sugar.

① Don't forget your change!
② The flight changed its route.
③ I change my car every three years.
④ Why don't you change your hair style?
⑤ His life definitely changed when he passed the test.

**B** 우리말과 일치하도록 〈보기〉에서 단어를 골라 문장을 완성하시오.

보기 stuff reduce diet come out

1 You must have a balanced ____________. 너는 균형 잡힌 식사를 해야 한다.
2 When will the new laptop computer ____________? 언제 새 노트북 컴퓨터가 나옵니까?
3 The company decided to ____________ annual spending. 회사는 연간 지출을 줄이기로 결정했다.
4 Special ____________ in this tea makes you feel better.
이 차 안에 있는 특별한 물질이 널 기분 좋게 만들어 준다.

## 4 Opinion

**A** 밑줄 친 단어와 비슷한 의미의 단어를 고르시오.

1 It is possible to build a house in a month.
① unlikely ② able ③ important ④ difficult ⑤ necessary

2 The mall is crowded with people.
① empty ② loose ③ full ④ cloudy ⑤ free

**B** 우리말과 일치하도록 〈보기〉에서 단어를 골라 문장을 완성하시오.

보기 get worse polluted besides blame

1 You always ____________ others. 너는 항상 남의 탓을 한다.
2 ____________, this movie is very educational for kids. 게다가 이 영화는 아이들에게 매우 교육적이다.
3 This river is ____________ with toxic waste from some factories.
이 강은 몇몇 공장에서 나온 유독성 폐기물로 오염되었다.
4 My grandma had an operation, but she seemed to ____________.
우리 할머니는 수술을 받았지만, 더욱 악화되는 것 같았다.

# 어휘 재충전

## 1 Letters

| | |
|---|---|
| □ amazing | a. 놀라운 |
| □ classmate | n. 반 친구 |
| □ get along with | ~와 잘 지내다 |
| □ seem | v. ~처럼 보이다 |
| □ a bit | 약간 |
| □ mean | a. 심술궂은 |
| □ stubborn | a. 고집불통인 |
| □ go into | ~을 시작하다 |
| □ argument | n. 논쟁, 말다툼 |
| □ have in common | 공통점이 있다 |
| □ brightly | ad. 밝게, 환하게 |
| □ hang out | (많은 시간을) 보내다 |
| □ jealousy | n. 질투심 |
| □ pity | n. 동정심 |

## 2 Psychology

| | |
|---|---|
| □ make a mistake | 실수하다 |
| □ likable | a. 호감이 가는 |
| □ mess up | 엉망으로 만들다 |
| □ draw | v. (사람의 마음을) 끌다 |
| □ support | v. 지지하다 |
| □ theory | n. 이론 |
| □ recording | n. 녹음 |
| □ contestant | n. 참가자 |
| □ knock over | 엎지르다 |
| □ spill | n. 쏟다, 엎지르다 |
| □ now and then | 가끔 |
| □ perfect | a. 완벽한 |
| □ likability | n. 호감도 |
| □ responsibility | n. 책임감 |
| □ ability | n. 능력 |
| □ politeness | n. 예의 바름, 정중함 |

## 3 Science

| | |
|---|---|
| □ poop | n. 대변 |
| □ global warming | 지구 온난화 |
| □ diet | n. 식사, 식품 |
| □ discover | v. 발견하다 |
| □ bamboo tree | n. 대나무 |
| □ change into | ~으로 변하다, 바뀌다 |
| □ sugar | n. 당분, 설탕 |
| □ stomach | n. 위 |
| □ turn A into B | A를 B로 바꾸다 |
| □ stuff | n. 물질 |
| □ a little bit of | 약간의, 조금의 |
| □ come out | 나오다 |
| □ lab | n. 실험실 |
| □ lots of | 많은 |
| □ instead of | ~ 대신에 |
| □ fossil fuel | 화석 연료 |
| □ reduce | v. 줄이다 |
| □ endangered | a. 멸종 위기에 처한 |

## 4 Opinion

| | |
|---|---|
| □ blame | v. 비난하다, 탓하다 |
| □ science fiction | 공상 과학 소설 |
| □ possible | a. 가능한 |
| □ planet | n. 행성 |
| □ the universe | 우주 |
| □ take care of | ~을 돌보다 |
| □ make a mess of | ~을 엉망으로 만들다 |
| □ clean up | 청소하다 |
| □ mess | n. 엉망인 상태 |
| □ crowded | a. 붐비는 |
| □ polluted | a. 오염된 |
| □ space | n. 공간 |
| □ natural disaster | 자연재해 |
| □ get worse | 악화되다 |
| □ kind of | 약간, 어느 정도 |
| □ flood | n. 홍수 |
| □ besides | ~외에, 게다가 |
| □ nevertheless | ad. ~에도 불구하고 |

# Chapter 07

Health

A bowl of cereal and milk is a favorite breakfast for millions. It's quick and tasty. But most brands of breakfast cereal have a dark secret. They are very high in sugar and fat and too low in fiber, vitamins, 5 and minerals. This may surprise you if you believe the ads for cereal. They always suggest that their company's product is really good for you. But most brands are less nutritious than chocolate cake and just as sweet. But don't worry. There are several breakfast cereals that are good for you. If you want to stay healthy and fit, you have to be a smart shopper 10 and read the cereal's nutrition label before you buy!

**1** 윗글의 내용에 맞게 빈칸에 들어갈 말이 바르게 짝지어진 것은?

Most brands of breakfast cereal are high in ________ and low in ________.

① fiber, sugar ② vitamins, minerals ③ fat, sugar
④ sugar, vitamins ⑤ minerals, fat

**2** 윗글에서 건강 유지를 위한 방법으로 언급한 것은?

① 시리얼을 하루에 한 번만 섭취하라.
② 구매 전에 쇼핑 목록을 작성하라.
③ 구매 전에 영양 성분표를 확인하라.
④ 표기된 영양 성분을 믿지 말라.
⑤ 브랜드를 잘 확인하고 음식을 섭취하라.

| | | |
|---|---|---|
| a bowl of ________ | cereal n. ________ | millions n. ________ |
| tasty a. ________ | secret n. ________ | fat n. ________ |
| fiber n. ________ | mineral n. ________ | surprise v. ________ |
| ad n. ________ | suggest v. ________ | nutritious a. ________ |
| just as ________ | several a. ________ | healthy a. ________ |
| fit a. ________ | shopper n. ________ | nutrition label ________ |

2
Letters

I'm writing about the book review of "Hurt Go Happy" by Ginny Rorby. It was in the February edition of your magazine. Although I'm a big fan of your magazine, I usually skip the book reviews. But last month, for some reason I decided to read this review. "Hurt Go Happy" sounded interesting, so I told my mom about the book, and she bought it for me. I read it last week, and I thought it was a great story. I especially liked Joey, the main character. She's deaf, but otherwise she's just like me. I'm a teenager, and I often feel left out and lonely. How lucky! She made a good friend. How amazing! She learned sign language from a clever chimpanzee! Thank you so much for the review! I recommended the book to my teacher for our school's library.

*Anna, 15, Huntsville, Alabama*

**1** 윗글의 목적으로 가장 알맞은 것은?

① 새로 발간된 잡지를 홍보하려고
② 구입한 책을 반품하려고
③ 서평에 대한 감사 인사를 하려고
④ 작가가 되기 위해 조언을 구하려고
⑤ 도서관에 비치할 책을 추천 받으려고

**2** Hurt Go Happy의 주인공에 관한 윗글의 내용과 일치하지 않는 것은?

① Joey라는 소녀이다.
② 청각 장애인이다.
③ 10대이다.
④ 외로웠지만, 다행히 친구를 사귀었다.
⑤ 침팬지에게 수화를 가르쳤다.

| | | |
|---|---|---|
| review n. ________ | edition n. ________ | magazine n. ________ |
| skip v. ________ | decide v. ________ | especially ad. ________ |
| main character ________ | deaf a. ________ | otherwise ad. ________ |
| feel left out ________ | lonely a. ________ | sign language n. ________ |
| clever a. ________ | chimpanzee n. ________ | recommend v. ________ |

Information

It's important to know exactly what you put into your body. By law, every food product approved by the Food and Drug Administration (FDA) must have a label on its package. The label says "Nutrition Facts," and it tells you exactly what the food contains. Let's check the label on a pack of potato chips. The particular label shows the total calories, fat, cholesterol, sodium, carbohydrate, protein, vitamins, and minerals per serving of chips. Pay attention to the "serving" size. It differs depending on the product. Here, it's 28 grams, about 12 chips. The label shows that there are 9 servings of chips in this container. So don't be fooled by the "140 calories." That's the calorie count of just one serving. If you eat the whole container of chips, you have just gained 1,260 calories!

**Nutrition Facts**
Serving Size 1 oz (28g/About 12 chips)
Servings Per Container About 9

| Amount per serving | |
|---|---|
| Calories 140 | Calories from Fat 60 |
| | % Daily Value |
| Total Fat 7g | 11% |
| Saturated Fat 1g | 5% |
| Trans Fat 0g | |
| Cholesterol 0mg | 0% |
| Sodium 170mg | 7% |
| Total Carbohydrate 18g | 6% |
| Dietary Fiber 1g | 4% |
| Sugars less than 1g | |
| Protein 2g | |
| Vitamin A 0% • | Vitamin C 0% |
| Calcium 2% • | Iron 2% |
| Vitamin E 4% • | Thiamin 2% |
| Riboflavin 2% • | Vitamin B6 4% |
| Phosphorus 6% • | Magnesium 4% |

*Food and Drug Administration 미국 식품의약국
*sodium 나트륨 *carbohydrate 탄수화물

**1** 윗글의 제목으로 가장 알맞은 것은?

① What Nutrition We Need
② What a Food Label Shows
③ How to Know the Serving Size
④ How to Classify Nutrition Facts
⑤ How Much Calories You Take per Day

| | | |
|---|---|---|
| law n. ______ | product n. ______ | approve v. ______ |
| label n. ______ | package n. ______ | nutrition fact ______ |
| contain v. ______ | pack n. ______ | particular a. ______ |
| calorie n. ______ | fat n. ______ | cholesterol n. ______ |
| protein n. ______ | mineral n. ______ | per prep. ______ |
| serving n. ______ | pay attention to ______ | differ v. ______ |
| depending on ______ | container n. ______ | be fooled by ______ |
| gain v. ______ | classify v. ______ | |

**2** 윗글에서 식품의 라벨에 표시된 내용으로 언급되지 않은 것은?

① 총 열량 ② 1회 제공량 ③ 수분 함유량
④ 지방 함유량 ⑤ 단백질 함유량

**3** 다음 식품 라벨을 읽고, 이 식품을 다 먹었을 경우 얼마의 열량을 얻게 되는지 고르시오.

**Nutrition Facts**
**Serving Size 12 g (About 10 chips)**
**Servings Per Container About 7**

| Amount for serving | % Daily Value |
|---|---|
| **Calories** 100 | |
| **Total Fat** 5 g | 9% |
| Saturated Fat 1 g | 3% |
| Trans Fat 0 g | |
| **Cholesterol** 0 mg | 0% |
| **Sodium** 130 mg | 5% |

① 84 calories
② 100 calories
③ 500 calories
④ 700 calories
⑤ 1200 calories

### 식품 법규

이물질 파동으로 식품 안전 문제가 대두됐던 2008년 이후, 식품과 관련하여 여러 법규가 정비되었다. 특히, 제품 성분, 제품명 표기, 원산지 표기 등에서 많은 변화가 생겼다. 예를 들어, 제품명에 표기되는 천연재료가 들어가지 않으면 'oo맛'이라는 표기를 할 수 없고, 대신 'oo향'이라고 표기해야 한다. 즉, 바나나 과즙이 들어가야만 '바나나맛 우유'라고 표기할 수 있고, 바나나 과즙이 들어가지 않으면 '바나나향 우유'라고 표기해야만 한다. 또한, 국내 농·축·수산업에서 재배 및 수확되는 모든 제품은 판매 시 원산지 표기를 반드시 명시해야 하며, 이를 위반할 경우 과징금을 부과한다.

Science

Do you like tea? Some cups of tea taste better than others. So, what's the secret to a delicious cup of tea? To answer the question, we need to look at air, water, and heat. Air and water mix together well at low temperatures, but they don't mix together very well at high temperatures. When a pot of water gets very hot, you can see lots of bubbles. The bubbles are air. The air is going out of the water. The longer the water bubbles and boils, the more it loses air. What does this have to do with the taste of tea? Water with more air in it makes tea taste better. So, to make the very best cup of tea, heat the water until it just starts to bubble. Then ______________ straight away, pour the water into a cup with tea, and enjoy!

| | | |
|---|---|---|
| tea n. ______ | secret n. ______ | delicious a. ______ |
| heat n. ______ | mix v. ______ | low a. ______ |
| temperature n. ______ | pot n. ______ | bubble n. ______ v. ______ |
| boil v. ______ | lose v. ______ | have to do with ______ |
| straight away ______ | pour v. ______ | flavor n. ______ |
| tea ceremony ______ | turn off ______ | take off ______ |
| turn on ______ | put on ______ | take out ______ |

**1** 윗글의 제목으로 가장 알맞은 것은?

① How to Buy Good Tca
② Why Tea Is Good for Health
③ Why We Learn Tea Ceremony
④ How to Make the Best Cup of Tea
⑤ How to Mix Together Air and Water

서술형

**2** 윗글의 빈칸에 들어갈 말로 가장 알맞은 것은?

① turn it off　② take it off　③ turn it on
④ put it on　⑤ take it out

**3** 윗글에서 다음 질문에 대한 답을 찾아 우리말로 쓰시오.

To make the best cup of tea, when do you have to turn off the heat?

______________________________________________

**이미지 맵** 글을 읽고, 빈칸을 완성하시오.

**Title**:
(1)__________________
__________________

- Air and water mix together well at low (2)____________.
- The longer the water (3)____________ and boils, the more it loses air.
- Water with more (4)____________ in it makes tea taste better.
- You must (5)____________ the water until it just starts to bubble.

# Review Test

## 1 Health

**A 빈칸에 들어갈 알맞은 단어를 고르시오.**

1 You should keep this ____________ and should not tell anyone.
너는 이 비밀을 지키고, 누구에게도 말하지 않아야 해.
① secret ② article ③ change ④ diary ⑤ word

2 She goes jogging every day to ____________ healthy.
그녀는 건강을 유지하기 위해 매일 조깅을 한다.
① feel ② stay ③ grow ④ leave ⑤ live

**B 우리말과 일치하도록 <보기>에서 단어를 골라 문장을 완성하시오.**

보기 nutritious several surprised a bowl of

1 Daniel has been sick for ____________ days. Daniel은 며칠 동안 아팠다.
2 She eats ____________ soup every morning. 그녀는 아침마다 수프 한 그릇을 먹는다.
3 It ____________ him that his friend moved to LA. 그는 친구가 LA로 이사를 가서 놀랐다.
4 Soybean is very ____________, but many children don't like it.
콩은 영양가가 높지만, 많은 아이들은 콩을 좋아하지 않는다.

## 2 Letters

**A 밑줄 친 단어와 반대되는 의미의 단어를 고르시오.**

1 He was so clever that he could solve the problem.
① wise ② brave ③ brilliant ④ smart ⑤ stupid

2 What made you decide to come to this party?
① discuss ② hesitate ③ choose ④ determine ⑤ consider

**B 우리말과 일치하도록 <보기>에서 단어를 골라 문장을 완성하시오.**

보기 deaf review skip lonely

1 I'll ____________ dinner to lose weight. 나는 살을 빼기 위해 저녁을 거를 거야.
2 He lives alone and sometimes feels ____________. 그는 혼자 살고 가끔 외롭다고 느낀다.
3 The book ____________ helped me choose the book. 그 서평은 내가 책을 고르는 데 도움이 되었다.
4 He is ____________ in his left ear after the accident.
그는 그 사고 이후로 왼쪽 귀가 들리지 않는다.

## 3 Information

**A** 다음 중 단어의 정의가 잘못된 것은?

① particular: ordinary or usual
② differ: to be unlike each other in some way
③ approve: to have a good opinion of something and accept it
④ container: something such as a box in which you can keep things
⑤ label: a piece of paper that gives you information about something

**B** 우리말과 일치하도록 〈보기〉에서 단어를 골라 문장을 완성하시오.

보기 fat contains calories gain law

1 At that time, Ben was a minor by ____________. 그 당시에, Ben은 법적으로 미성년자였다.
2 I'm counting ____________ because I'm on a diet. 나는 다이어트 중이어서 칼로리를 계산한다.
3 She always eats foods which are low in ____________. 그녀는 항상 지방이 적은 음식을 먹는다.
4 You must eat food that ____________ lots of minerals. 미네랄이 많이 함유된 음식을 먹어야 한다.
5 He tried to ____________ experience during the vacation.
그는 방학 동안 경험을 쌓기 위해 노력했다.

## 4 Science

**A** 밑줄 친 단어와 비슷한 의미의 단어를 고르시오.

1 Then, mix the egg and sugar in a bowl.
① bake ② boil ③ fix ④ blend ⑤ add

2 The food you made for dinner was really delicious.
① spicy ② tasty ③ expensive ④ favorite ⑤ special

**B** 우리말과 일치하도록 〈보기〉에서 단어를 골라 문장을 완성하시오.

보기 turn off temperature straight away bubble

1 He found the answer ____________. 그는 즉시 답을 알아차렸다.
2 Don't forget to ____________ your cell phone. 휴대 전화 끄는 것을 잊지 마.
3 When the milk begins to ____________, add vinegar. 우유에 거품이 생기기 시작할 때 식초를 넣어라.
4 If you want to use the air conditioner, you should set the ____________ at 25 degrees.
에어컨을 사용하고 싶다면, 온도를 25도에 맞춰야 한다.

# 어휘 재충전

## 1 Health

- □ a bowl of 한 그릇의
- □ cereal n. 시리얼
- □ millions n. 수백만
- □ tasty a. 맛있는
- □ secret n. 비밀, 기밀
- □ fat n. 지방
- □ fiber n. 섬유질
- □ mineral n. 무기질
- □ surprise v. 놀라게 하다
- □ ad n. 광고
- □ suggest v. 제안하다, 암시하다
- □ nutritious a. 영양분이 많은
- □ just as 꼭 ~처럼
- □ several a. 몇몇의
- □ healthy a. 건강한
- □ fit a. 건강한, 탄탄한
- □ shopper n. 쇼핑객
- □ nutrition label 영양 성분표

## 2 Letters

- □ review n. 논평, 비평
- □ edition n. 판, 호
- □ magazine n. 잡지
- □ skip v. 건너뛰다
- □ decide v. 결정하다
- □ especially ad. 특히
- □ main character 주인공
- □ deaf a. 청각 장애가 있는
- □ otherwise ad. 다른 점에서는
- □ feel left out 소외감을 느끼다
- □ lonely a. 외로운, 쓸쓸한
- □ sign language n. 수화
- □ clever a. 영리한, 똑똑한
- □ chimpanzee n. 침팬지
- □ recommend v. 추천하다

## 3 Information

- □ law n. 법
- □ product n. 상품, 제품
- □ approve v. 승인하다
- □ label n. 표, 라벨
- □ package n. 포장, 상자
- □ nutrition fact 영양 성분
- □ contain v. 함유하다
- □ pack n. 봉지, 포장 꾸러미
- □ particular a. 특별한, 특정한
- □ calorie n. 열량, 칼로리
- □ fat n. 지방
- □ cholesterol n. 콜레스테롤
- □ protein n. 단백질
- □ mineral n. 무기질
- □ per prep. ~마다
- □ serving n. 1인분, 1회 분량
- □ pay attention to ~에 주목하다
- □ differ v. 다르다
- □ depending on ~에 따라
- □ container n. 그릇, 용기
- □ be fooled by ~에 속다
- □ gain v. 얻다
- □ classify v. 구분하다

## 4 Science

- □ tea n. 홍차, 차
- □ secret n. 비밀, 비법
- □ delicious a. 맛있는
- □ heat n. 온도, 열
- □ mix v. 섞이다
- □ low a. 낮은
- □ temperature n. 온도
- □ pot n. 냄비, 솥
- □ bubble n. 거품 v. 거품이 일다
- □ boil v. 끓다
- □ lose v. 잃다, 줄다
- □ have to do with ~와 관계가 있다
- □ straight away 즉시
- □ pour v. 붓다, 따르다
- □ flavor n. 맛
- □ tea ceremony 다도(차를 마실 때의 예의범절)
- □ turn off (전기, 가스 등을) 끄다
- □ take off ~을 벗다, 이륙하다
- □ turn on ~을 켜다
- □ put on ~을 입다
- □ take out ~을 꺼내다

# Chapter 08

Life

Researchers studied the relationship between happiness and people's conversations. Volunteers wore automatic speech recorders for four days. The researchers listened to every conversation recorded and classified each as either "meaningful" or "small talk." They also tested each volunteer's general mood. They discovered that happiness relates strongly to ______(A)______ time alone and ______(B)______ time talking. In fact, the happiest volunteers spent 25 percent less time alone and 70 percent more time talking than the unhappiest participants. There was a difference in conversation styles, too. The happiest volunteers had twice as many meaningful discussions and one third as much small talk as the unhappiest volunteers. It seems that meaningful conversation makes for more happiness than small talk does.

**1** 윗글의 주제로 가장 알맞은 것은?

① 혼자 보내는 시간이 많을수록 삶이 여유롭다.
② 행복과 사람들의 대화 사이에는 연관성이 없다.
③ 대화 방식에 관계없이 대화를 많이 하면 행복함을 느낀다.
④ 의미 있는 대화를 많이 할수록 사람들은 행복함을 느낀다.
⑤ 잡담을 많이 하는 것보다는 혼자서 시간을 보내는 것이 낫다.

**2** 윗글의 빈칸 (A)와 (B)에 들어갈 말로 바르게 짝지어진 것은?

① more – less ② worse – less ③ more – more
④ better – more ⑤ less – more

| | | |
|---|---|---|
| relationship n. ______ | happiness n. ______ | conversation n. ______ |
| volunteer n. ______ | automatic a. ______ | recorder n. ______ |
| classify v. ______ | meaningful a. ______ | small talk ______ |
| general a. ______ | mood n. ______ | discover v. ______ |
| relate to ______ | participant n. ______ | discussion n. ______ |

2

Health

We know that laughing is healthy. But how exactly does it help to improve health? Here are five ways that laughter works for you. First, it produces health-giving hormones and reduces harmful ones. This helps your body fight diseases. Second, it provides a physical and emotional release. In other words, it helps you "let off steam." Don't you feel refreshed after a really good laugh? That's because your body released stress. Third, it's a good workout. It works muscles in your belly, chest, and back. Fourth, it's a distraction. You can't focus on negative thoughts when you're laughing. And fifth, it changes your point of view. Problems seem smaller and less scary when you can joke and laugh about them. So let's lighten up and ______________________ in our lives.

*health-giving hormone 건강을 증진시키는 호르몬

**1** 윗글의 주제로 가장 알맞은 것은?

① why people want to live longer
② how laughing affects your health
③ the emotional effect of laughing
④ how to relieve stress
⑤ what makes you get stressed

**2** 윗글의 빈칸에 들어갈 말로 가장 알맞은 것은?

① go and get some rest
② earn a lot of money
③ get some exercise
④ get a good night's sleep
⑤ find more humor and fun

| | | |
|---|---|---|
| improve v. ______ | laughter n. ______ | produce v. ______ |
| reduce v. ______ | harmful a. ______ | disease n. ______ |
| provide v. ______ | physical a. ______ | emotional a. ______ |
| release n. ______ | in other words ______ | let off steam ______ |
| refreshed a. ______ | workout n. ______ | belly n. ______ |
| distraction n. ______ | point of view ______ | lighten up ______ |

Sports

For five months of the year, the National Football League takes over Sundays in America. On Sundays, more people watch NFL games than go to church. When you see NFL games on TV, it's hard to understand why they are so popular. Sometimes NFL game lasts around 3 hours and 12 minutes. But the real game time when the players are actually in action is just 11 minutes. Indeed, the average NFL broadcast has more replays (17 minutes) than live play (11 minutes). And around 75 minutes is nothing but the players, coaches, and referees hanging around on the field. Of course when it's on TV, it's not just about the game. It's about advertising, too. An average broadcast includes 20 commercial breaks containing around 100 ads. This takes up an hour. That is about one third of the game.

| | | |
|---|---|---|
| take over ______ | last v. ______ | around ad. ______ |
| in action ______ | indeed ad. ______ | average a. ______ |
| broadcast n. ______ | replay n. ______ | nothing but ______ |
| referee n. ______ | hang around ______ | commercial break n. ______ |
| contain v. ______ | take up ______ | |

**1** **NFL에 관한 윗글의 내용과 일치하지 않는 것은?**

① NFL 시즌에는 교회에 가는 사람보다 경기를 보는 사람이 더 많다.

② 경기에서 선수들이 실제로 뛰는 시간은 11분에 불과하다.

③ 미식축구 방송은 실제 경기보다 다시 보기에 할애하는 시간이 더 많다.

④ 사람들은 TV로 시청하는 것보다 경기장에서 미식축구 경기를 보는 것을 선호한다.

⑤ 미식축구 방송에는 100편의 광고 방송이 포함되어 있다.

**2** **윗글에 따르면 미식축구 방송에서 광고에 할애하는 시간은 얼마인가?**

① 11분　　② 17분　　③ 60분

④ 75분　　⑤ 100분

**3** **윗글에서 알맞은 말을 찾아 다음 요약문을 완성하시오.**

When an NFL game is on TV, it's not only about the
_____________ but also about _____________.

**미식축구(NFL)**

미식축구 경기는 15분씩 4번의 쿼터(quarter)로 구성이 되며, 각 쿼터별로 획득한 점수를 합산하여 많은 점수를 얻은 팀이 이긴다. 1, 2쿼터를 전반으로, 3, 4쿼터를 후반으로 나누며, 전반이 끝난 후 20분간의 하프타임이 주어진다. 2쿼터와 4쿼터에서는 끝나기 2분 전에 '2분의 경고 시간'이 주어진다. 순수 경기 시간은 1시간이지만 특정한 경우에는 경기 시간을 멈추기 때문에 실제 경기시간은 3시간 정도 소요된다. 경기 시간이 멈추는 경우는 다음과 같다.

- ◆ 반칙이 일어났을 경우
- ◆ 선수 부상 및 기타 문제 발생 시 심판의 타임아웃
- ◆ 공을 든 선수가 사이드라인 밖으로 나갔을 경우
- ◆ 패스 플레이가 실패할 경우
- ◆ 전반, 후반 각각 팀당 3번의 타임아웃

4쿼터 이후에도 양팀이 동점일 경우에는 15분간의 연장 경기를 진행한다.

Science

Are you a morning person, an evening person, or somewhere in between? You probably already know that you have good times and not-so-good times to study and work. Your brain works best in the morning if you're a 5 morning-type, and a night owl's brain works best at night. It's obvious, isn't it? Well, no. It's not that simple. New research shows that you actually think more creatively when you're tired. It's because a tired brain cannot focus easily on one thing. (the time, think of, were, you, in class, when, very tired). You tried hard to pay attention, but it was 10 impossible. Too many other thoughts, ideas, and feelings interrupted you. According to the research, these interruptions create unusual connections. The unusual connections among ideas lead to creativity. Your brain connects unrelated thoughts, and suddenly you may think, "Aha! What a wonderful idea!"

*a night owl 올빼미 족

| | | |
|---|---|---|
| somewhere ad. | in between | probably ad. |
| work v. | obvious a. | creatively ad. |
| focus on | easily ad. | think of |
| pay attention | impossible a. | interrupt v. |
| interruption n. | unusual a. | connection n. |
| lead to | creativity n. | connect v. |
| unrelated a. | | |

**1** 윗글의 제목으로 가장 알맞은 것은?

① The Power of the Human Brain
② A Tired Brain's Creative Ideas
③ The Features of Creative People
④ Research about Personal Habits
⑤ A Morning Person and an Evening Person

**2** 윗글의 내용과 일치하면 T, 그렇지 않으면 F를 쓰시오.

(1) 새로운 연구에 따르면, 피곤할 때 더 창의적이다. ________
(2) 지친 뇌는 한 가지에 쉽게 집중할 수 없다. ________
(3) 지친 뇌를 깨우려면 더 많은 생각이 필요하다. ________

서술형

**3** 윗글의 ( ) 안에 주어진 단어를 우리말에 맞게 배열하여 문장을 완성하시오.

당신이 수업 중에 매우 피곤했던 때를 생각해 봐라.

________________________________________

이미지 맵 글을 읽고, 빈칸을 완성하시오.

**Title**:
(1)________________
________________

Research says that you are creative when you're (2)__________.

A tired brain can't (3)__________ one thing easily.

Many thoughts, ideas, and feelings can (4)__________ you.

The interruptions create unusual (5)__________.

The unusual connections lead to (6)__________.

# Review Test

**1** Life

**A** 밑줄 친 단어와 반대되는 의미의 단어를 고르시오.

1 The necklace is very meaningful to me.
① important ② minor ③ valuable ④ worth ⑤ major

2 They wish each other happiness and good luck.
① wealth ② kindness ③ freedom ④ misery ⑤ satisfaction

**B** 주어진 뜻에 알맞은 단어를 〈보기〉에서 찾아 쓰시오.

보기 classify participant discussion discover volunteer

1 an activity in which people talk about something ____________
2 to find something, especially for the first time ____________
3 to divide things into groups ____________
4 a person who does something without being paid ____________
5 a person who takes part in an activity ____________

**2** Health

**A** 밑줄 친 단어와 반대되는 의미의 단어를 고르시오.

1 Do you want to improve your driving skill?
① advance ② decrease ③ boost ④ increase ⑤ promote

2 Playing computer games for too long can be harmful to teens.
① helpful ② painful ③ unsafe ④ damaging ⑤ dangerous

**B** 우리말과 일치하도록 〈보기〉에서 단어를 골라 문장을 완성하시오.

보기 distraction release reduce point of view

1 Taking a deep breath helps you to ____________ stress.
숨을 깊게 들이마시는 것은 스트레스를 줄이는 데 도움이 된다.

2 Using smart phones can be a ____________ in the library.
도서관에서 스마트폰의 사용은 방해가 될 수 있습니다.

3 I understand your ______________, but I can't agree with you.
나는 너의 관점을 이해하지만 동의할 수는 없다.

4 The kidnapper demanded $10,000 for the ____________ of the girl.
유괴범은 소녀를 풀어주는 데 만 달러를 요구했다.

## 3 Sports

### A 〈보기〉의 밑줄 친 live와 같은 의미로 쓰인 것은?

보기 NFL broadcast has more replays than live play.

① I live with my grandparents.
② How long have you lived here?
③ Plants cannot live without water.
④ The band performed a live concert.
⑤ The movie star lives on the seventh floor.

### B 우리말과 일치하도록 〈보기〉에서 단어를 골라 문장을 완성하시오.

보기 last  average  including  nothing but

1 I want ____________ summer vacation. 나는 단지 여름 휴가를 원한다.
2 They work an ____________ of 8 hours a day. 그들은 하루에 평균 8시간 일한다.
3 Some Indian movies ____________ over three hours. 몇몇 인도 영화들은 3시간이 넘는다.
4 You have to pay $400 per month ____________ utilities.
당신은 공과금을 포함하여 매달 400달러를 지불해야 한다.

## Science

### A 밑줄 친 단어와 비슷한 의미의 단어를 고르시오.

1 It is obvious that we will win the game.
① clear ② doubtful ③ dull ④ hidden ⑤ uncertain

2 It is impossible to pass the exam.
① reasonable ② practical ③ believable ④ hopeless ⑤ imaginable

### B 우리말과 일치하도록 〈보기〉에서 단어를 골라 문장을 완성하시오.

보기 focus on  think of  connect  interrupt

1 Don't ____________ me when I'm on vacation. 내가 휴가 중일 때는 나를 방해하지 마세요.
2 What do you ____________ the new math teacher? 새로 온 수학 선생님에 대해 어떻게 생각합니까?
3 With all the noise, Sally can't ____________ working. 소음 때문에 Sally는 일에 집중할 수 없다.
4 Enter the password to ____________ to other computers.
다른 컴퓨터에 연결하려면 비밀번호를 입력하세요.

# 어휘 재충전

## 1 Life

- □ relationship n. 관계
- □ happiness n. 행복
- □ conversation n. 대화
- □ volunteer n. 지원자, 자원봉사자
- □ automatic a. 자동의
- □ recorder n. 녹음기
- □ classify v. 분류하다
- □ meaningful a. 중요한
- □ small talk 잡담
- □ general a. 전반적인
- □ mood n. 기분
- □ discover v. 발견하다
- □ relate to ~과 관련이 있다
- □ participant n. 참가자
- □ discussion n. 논의, 상의

## 2 Health

- □ improve v. 개선하다
- □ laughter n. 웃음
- □ produce v. 생산하다
- □ reduce v. 줄이다
- □ harmful a. 해로운
- □ disease n. 질병
- □ provide v. 제공하다
- □ physical a. 육체의, 신체적인
- □ emotional a. 정서상의, 감정적인
- □ release n. 해방(감), 석방
- □ in other words 즉, 다시 말해서
- □ let off steam 울분을 발산하다
- □ refreshed a. 상쾌한
- □ workout n. 운동
- □ belly n. 복부
- □ distraction n. 주의가 흩어짐, 기분전환
- □ point of view 관점
- □ lighten up 기운 내다, 가볍게 생각하다

## 3 Sports

- □ take over 떠맡다, 점거하다
- □ last v. 계속되다
- □ around ad. 약, 대략
- □ in action 활동하는
- □ indeed ad. 정말로, 사실은
- □ average a. 평균의
- □ broadcast n. 방송
- □ replay n. 다시 보기
- □ nothing but 단지, 다름이 아니라
- □ referee n. 심판
- □ hang around 배회하다
- □ commercial break n. 광고를 위한 프로 중단 시간
- □ contain v. ~이 들어 있다
- □ take up 차지하다

## 4 Science

- □ somewhere ad. 어딘가에
- □ in between 중간에
- □ probably ad. 아마도
- □ work v. 일하다, 작동하다
- □ obvious a. 분명한
- □ creatively ad. 창의적으로
- □ focus on ~에 집중하다
- □ easily ad. 쉽게
- □ think of ~을 생각하다
- □ pay attention 주의를 기울이다
- □ impossible a. 불가능한
- □ interrupt v. 방해하다
- □ interruption n. 방해
- □ unusual a. 흔치 않은, 드문
- □ connection n. 연결, 관련
- □ lead to ~로 이어지다
- □ creativity n. 창의력, 독창성
- □ connect v. 연결하다
- □ unrelated a. 관련 없는

# Chapter 09

People
Health
Economy
Language
note
notebook
Fighting!
remocon
remote control

People

She was born in England in 1775 and began writing stories as a young child. Her six novels remain bestsellers today — 200 years after she wrote them. *Emma, Pride and Prejudice, Mansfield Park, Northanger Abbey, Sense and Sensibility*, and *Persuasion* have been made into many movies and TV series. The stories are romantic, but gently make fun of the strict morals and customs of life in rural England at the time. She disliked cities and rarely traveled far from home. Only four of her novels were published during her lifetime, and they were published anonymously. When she died at the age of 41, only her family knew she was a successful novelist. Now, the whole world knows her name, Jane Austen.

**1** **Jane Austen에 관한 윗글의 내용과 일치하지 않는 것은?**

① 1775년에 영국에서 태어났다.
② 소설 속에서 영국의 시골 모습을 담아냈다.
③ 생전에 6개의 작품만이 출판되었다.
④ 여행을 떠난 적이 거의 없다.
⑤ 그녀의 작품이 영화와 TV 시리즈로 만들어졌다.

**2** **Jane Austen이 생전에 성공한 소설가로 알려지지 않은 이유로 가장 알맞은 것은?**

① 익명으로 책을 출판해서
② 작품의 수가 적어서
③ 여성 작가여서
④ 생전에 출판된 작품이 없어서
⑤ 시골에 살고 있어서

| | | |
|---|---|---|
| novel n. ______ | remain v. ______ | pride n. ______ |
| prejudice n. ______ | abbey n. ______ | sense n. ______ |
| sensibility n. ______ | persuasion n. ______ | series n. ______ |
| gently ad. ______ | make fun of ______ | strict a. ______ |
| moral n. ______ | custom n. ______ | rural a. ______ |
| rarely ad. ______ | publish v. ______ | lifetime n. ______ |
| anonymously ad. ______ | successful a. ______ | novelist n. ______ |

2
Health

We all know that we should brush our teeth regularly to keep them healthy. But did you know that brushing too soon after eating or drinking does more harm than good? According to the Australian Dental Association, it's particularly harmful to brush your teeth soon after drinking cola or orange juice. It's because these drinks have a lot of acid. Acid makes your teeth weak, so your toothbrush easily scratches your teeth when you brush your teeth. You should wait at least 30 minutes after eating or drinking before you brush. You need this much time to make enough saliva. The saliva will protect your teeth like armor. Remember that you need to ______________________ to keep them strong.

*acid 산성, 산도 *saliva 침

**1** 윗글의 주제로 가장 알맞은 것은?

① 산이 치아에 미치는 영향 ② 올바른 양치질 시간 ③ 탄산음료의 위험성
④ 충치를 예방하는 방법 ⑤ 치약과 치아 건강의 관계

**2** 윗글의 빈칸에 들어갈 말로 가장 알맞은 것은?

① brush your teeth for three minutes
② brush your teeth right after meals
③ give your teeth a break after meals
④ brush your teeth with a soft toothbrush
⑤ brush your teeth three times a day

| | | |
|---|---|---|
| regularly ad. ________ | dental a. ________ | association n. ________ |
| particularly ad. ________ | harmful a. ________ | brush one's teeth ________ |
| weak a. ________ | toothbrush n. ________ | scratch v. ________ |
| at least ________ | protect v. ________ | armor n. ________ |
| break n. ________ | meal n. ________ | |

Economy

I'm a twenty-year-old American student from New York. Every day, I have a Big Mac and a Starbucks latte for lunch. It always costs $8.90. The burger is $4.60, and the coffee is $4.30. Today, as usual, I took $10 and went out to buy my favorite lunch. But I didn't have enough money! Can you guess why? I'm not in New York any more. I'm in Switzerland now! McDonalds and Starbucks are in every country now. No matter where you are, the Big Mac and Starbucks latte always taste the same. The only difference is the price. It changes from country to country. It's exactly the same food, but the price is much different. Can you guess how much I need for my favorite lunch in Switzerland? $6.80 for the burger and $7.10 for the latte. It's expensive to live in Switzerland.

| | | |
|---|---|---|
| latte n. ________ | cost v. ________ | as usual ________ |
| enough a. ________ | guess v. ________ | Switzerland n. ________ |
| no matter where ________ | taste v. ________ | difference n. ________ |
| price n. ________ | exactly ad. ________ | expensive a. ________ |

**1** 윗글의 내용과 일치하면 T, 그렇지 않으면 F를 쓰시오.

(1) 나는 햄버거와 커피를 점심으로 먹는다. ________

(2) 맥도날드의 햄버거는 세계 어디에서든 가격이 동일하다. ________

(3) 나는 현재 가지고 있는 돈으로 점심을 먹을 수 없다. ________

**2** 윗글에 따르면 필자가 스위스에서 미국에서와 같은 점심을 먹으려면 얼마가 필요한가?

① $7.10 ② $8.90 ③ $11.70
④ $13.90 ⑤ $15.00

서술형

**3** 윗글에서 알맞은 말을 찾아 다음 요약문을 완성하시오.

Although a Big Mac and a Starbucks latte ____________ the same in America as in Switzerland, the ____________ is different. Living in Switzerland is more ____________ than living in America.

**빅맥지수(Big Mac Index)**

빅맥지수는 영국의 경제전문지 이코노미스트(The Economist)에서 매년 세계 120국에서 판매되는 빅맥 햄버거의 가격을 달러로 환산해 분기마다 한 번씩 발표하는 지수이다. 미국 맥도날드 사의 햄버거 제품인 빅맥을 기준으로 하기 때문에 이러한 이름이 붙었다. 빅맥과 같이 품질이나 크기, 재료가 모두 표준화된 제품은 각국의 물가를 비교하기에 좋은 기준이 된다. 세계적으로 널리 쓰이는 제품이 얼마에 팔리는지 알면, 그 나라의 통화 가치도 쉽게 비교할 수 있다. 미국의 빅맥지수 외에도 세계적으로 많이 팔리는 특정 제품 중 스타벅스의 카페라떼 그란데(중간) 사이즈를 각 나라별 달러로 환산한 라떼지수도 있다.

Language

Hundreds of English words are used in everyday Korean. But some words don't mean the same thing in both languages. We call them "Konglish false friends" because they cause big problems when Koreans and native English speakers need to speak to each other in English. (easily confuse, here are, a few, that, us, words.)

What's a "note"? You may be writing in one right now! But that's a "notebook" in English, and a "note" is a short written message. If you ask native English speakers for a note, they will be very confused.

"Fighting" is a favorite Korean expression of encouragement. But you can't use it that way in English. It only means being in a physical fight or argument with someone else. As in, "My brothers are fighting over the remote control." Speaking of the remote control, native English speakers have no idea what a "remocon" is. They only say "remote control" or "remote" for short. There are many more Konglish false friends. Don't let them fool you when you're using English!

*false friend (두 언어 사이에서) 비슷해 보이지만 의미하는 바가 다른 단어

| | | |
|---|---|---|
| hundreds of ______ | mean v. ______ | false a. ______ |
| cause v. ______ | confuse v. ______ | native a. ______ |
| written a. ______ | encouragement n. ______ | physical a. ______ |
| argument n. ______ | as in ______ | fight over ______ |
| speaking of ______ | remote control ______ | for short ______ |
| let v. ______ | fool v. ______ | originated from ______ |

**1** 윗글의 제목으로 가장 알맞은 것은?

① The Most Common Error in Korean
② Broken English from False Friends
③ How to Memorize English Words
④ English Words Originated from Latin
⑤ Differences between Korean and English

**2** Konglish false friends에 관한 윗글의 내용과 일치하지 않는 것은?

① Remocon은 잘못된 영어 표현이다.
② Remote는 remote control의 줄임말이다.
③ Fighting은 한국에서 격려의 의미로 쓰인다.
④ Fighting은 본래 몸싸움이나 언쟁을 의미한다.
⑤ Notebook은 영어에서 짧은 메시지를 의미한다.

**3** 윗글의 (　) 안에 주어진 단어를 바르게 배열하여 문장을 완성하시오.

_______________________________________________

글을 읽고, 빈칸을 완성하시오.

**Title**: (1)______________________________

Some words don't mean the (2)___________ thing in Korean and English.

| | | |
|---|---|---|
| "Note" is not the same as "notebook." "Note" means a short written (3)___________ in English. | "Fighting" is used for expression of (4)______________ in Korea. "Fighting" means a physical fight or (5)___________ in English. | "Remote" is short for (6)_____________. "Remocon" is not used in English-speaking countries. |

# Review Test

## 1 People

**A 빈칸에 알맞은 단어를 고르시오.**

1 They will ____________ the book in English. 그들은 그 책을 영어로 출간할 것이다.
① tell ② publish ③ draw ④ establish ⑤ persuade

2 Islamic countries have ____________ rules about people's clothes.
이슬람 국가에는 의복에 관한 엄격한 법규가 있다.
① polite ② loose ③ strict ④ generous ⑤ successful

**B 우리말과 일치하도록 〈보기〉에서 단어를 골라 문장을 완성하시오.**

보기 gently successful rural novelist

1 Many people have moved into ____________ areas. 많은 사람들이 시골로 이사를 갔다.
2 I ____________ covered the puppy up with a blanket. 나는 담요로 강아지를 부드럽게 감쌌다.
3 The ____________ is well known for her wit and humor. 그 소설가는 재치와 유머로 유명하다.
4 The surprise party I gave for him was very ____________.
내가 그를 위해 열어 준 깜짝 파티는 매우 성공적이었다.

## 2 Health

**A 밑줄 친 단어와 반대되는 의미의 단어를 고르시오.**

1 My whole body felt <u>weak</u>.
① poor ② mighty ③ fine ④ safe ⑤ light

2 She doesn't have <u>enough</u> experience in this field.
① lacking ② little ③ any ④ a lot of ⑤ too much

**B 우리말과 일치하도록 〈보기〉에서 단어를 골라 문장을 완성하시오.**

보기 particularly break scratched at least

1 Jessica needed a ____________ from her work. Jessica는 일로부터 휴식이 필요했다.
2 The dog ____________ the door the whole night through. 강아지는 밤새도록 문을 긁었다.
3 You should arrive ____________ 30 minutes before departure.
적어도 출발 30분 전에 도착해야 한다.
4 It is ____________ important for people with heart trouble.
그것은 심장병이 있는 사람들에게 특히 중요하다.

정답 및 해설 p27

## 3 Economy

### A 〈보기〉의 밑줄 친 costs와 같은 의미로 쓰인 것은?

보기 The lunch always costs $8.90.

① It cost me lots of labor.
② He had to win at any cost.
③ The mistake cost him his job.
④ How much does this book cost?
⑤ The earthquake cost hundreds of lives.

### B 우리말과 일치하도록 〈보기〉에서 단어를 골라 문장을 완성하시오.

보기 difference　exactly　guess　as usual

1 Can you ____________ why he didn't come? 그가 왜 안 왔는지 추측할 수 있겠니?
2 She goes to school by subway ____________. 그녀는 늘 그렇듯이 지하철을 타고 학교를 간다.
3 I don't know the ____________ between the two words. 나는 그 두 단어의 차이점을 모르겠다.
4 Could you explain ____________ what happened?
무슨 일이 있었는지 정확히 설명해 줄 수 있나요?

## 4 Language

### A 밑줄 친 단어와 비슷한 의미의 단어를 고르시오.

1 I had an argument with my sister this morning.
①apology　②praise　③conversation　④debate　⑤understanding

2 The letter was a great encouragement to me.
①conflict　②support　③confidence　④concern　⑤delight

### B 우리말과 일치하도록 〈보기〉에서 단어를 골라 문장을 완성하시오.

보기 for short　physical　fight over　confuse

1 They always ____________ little things. 그들은 항상 사소한 일로 싸운다.
2 Most teens go through ____________ changes. 청소년 대부분이 신체적 변화를 겪는다.
3 I sometimes ____________ him with his twin brother. 나는 가끔 그와 쌍둥이 동생을 혼동한다.
4 His name is Benjamin, and we call him Ben ____________.
그의 이름은 Benjamin이고, 우리는 줄여서 Ben이라고 부른다.

# 어휘 재충전

## 1 People

- □ novel n. 소설
- □ remain v. 계속 ~이다
- □ pride n. 자존심, 오만
- □ prejudice n. 편견, 선입견
- □ abbey n. 대사원
- □ sense n. 감각, 판단력
- □ sensibility n. 감성, 예민함
- □ persuasion n. 설득
- □ series n. 연속, 시리즈
- □ gently ad. 부드럽게, 완만하게
- □ make fun of ~을 놀리다, 비웃다
- □ strict a. 엄격한
- □ moral n. 도덕(률)
- □ custom n. 관습
- □ rural a. 시골의
- □ rarely ad. 좀처럼 ~않는
- □ publish v. 출판하다
- □ lifetime n. 일생, 평생
- □ anonymously ad. 익명으로
- □ successful a. 성공한
- □ novelist n. 소설가

## 2 Health

- □ regularly ad. 규칙적으로
- □ dental a. 치아의
- □ association n. 협회
- □ particularly ad. 특히
- □ harmful a. 해로운, 유해한
- □ brush one's teeth 칫솔질하다
- □ weak a. 약한
- □ toothbrush n. 칫솔
- □ scratch v. 긁다
- □ at least 적어도, 최소한
- □ protect v. 보호하다
- □ armor n. 갑옷, 철갑
- □ break n. 휴식, 중단
- □ meal n. 식사

## 3 Economy

- □ latte n. 라테(우유를 탄 에스프레소 커피)
- □ cost v. (값이) ~이다
- □ as usual 평소처럼
- □ enough a. 충분한
- □ guess v. 추측하다
- □ Switzerland n. 스위스
- □ no matter where 어디를 가더라도
- □ taste v. 맛이 나다
- □ difference n. 차이, 다름
- □ price n. 가격
- □ exactly ad. 정확히
- □ expensive a. 비싼, 비용이 많이 드는

## 4 Language

- □ hundreds of 수백의
- □ mean v. 의미하다
- □ false a. 가짜의, 거짓의
- □ cause v. ~을 야기하다
- □ confuse v. 혼란시키다
- □ native a. 모국의, 타고난
- □ written a. 글로 표현된
- □ encouragement n. 격려
- □ physical a. 육체의, 신체의
- □ argument n. 논쟁, 언쟁
- □ as in ~의 경우와 같이
- □ fight over ~에 관하여 싸우다
- □ speaking of ~에 관해 말한다면
- □ remote control 리모컨
- □ for short 줄여서, 생략하여
- □ let v. ~하게 두다
- □ fool v. 속이다, 기만하다
- □ originated from ~에서 유래한

# Chapter 10

# 1 Art

A dust artist?!

Rafael is an artist. He draws and paints very well. People love the pictures he makes. But there's something unusual about Rafael and his art. The thing is that he draws and creates pictures without using paint or a brush. Then, what does he use to create his works of art? He draws in the dust on cars. Rafael uses his fingers and moves them around in the dust on a car. His fingers make lines in the dust, and beautiful buildings and birds appear on the car. The pictures look so cool. People leave their dusty cars at the car park where Rafael works. They want Rafael to draw on them. For the small price of a parking fee, they get a wonderful work of art.

**1** 윗글에서 Rafael이 그림을 그릴 때 사용한 도구로 언급된 것은?

① paint ② brush ③ fingers
④ hair ⑤ feather

**2** 윗글에서 사람들이 Rafael에게 그림에 대한 대가로 지불한 것을 찾아 영어로 쓰시오.

______________________________

| | | |
|---|---|---|
| unusual a. ______ | create v. ______ | without prep. ______ |
| paint n. ______ | brush n. ______ | work n. ______ |
| dust n. ______ | appear v. ______ | leave v. ______ |
| dusty a. ______ | car park ______ | parking fee ______ |

Humor

Mr. and Mrs. Smith planned a holiday in Mexico. But Mrs. Smith had to finish a job in New York. So, they agreed to meet at their hotel, and Mr. Smith traveled ahead. When he arrived, he sent a quick email to his wife. However, he hit a key by mistake when he typed the address. The message never reached Mrs. Smith. Instead, it went to the wife of an old preacher. The preacher was the kind who always preached about hell. He had only just died the day before. The widow checked her email and screamed. Her daughters came running and found their mother on the floor. Then they looked at her computer and saw this message on the screen:

My darling wife, I can't wait for you to come down.

P.S. It's a lot hotter down here.

**1** 윗글의 내용과 일치하지 않는 것은?

① Smith 부인은 남편과 함께 출발할 수 없었다.
② 목사님은 항상 지옥에 관한 설교를 했다.
③ 미망인은 남편이 보낸 이메일을 읽고 기절했다.
④ Smith 씨는 이메일 주소를 잘못 입력했다.
⑤ Smith 부인은 Smith 씨의 이메일을 받지 못했다.

**2** 윗글에서 목사의 미망인이 느꼈을 심정으로 가장 알맞은 것은?

① 안도 ② 낙담 ③ 절망 ④ 공포 ⑤ 후회

| | | |
|---|---|---|
| plan v. ______ | agree v. ______ | ahead ad. ______ |
| quick a. ______ | key n. ______ | by mistake ______ |
| type v. ______ | reach v. ______ | instead ad. ______ |
| preacher n. ______ | kind n. ______ | preach v. ______ |
| hell n. ______ | the day before ______ | widow n. ______ |

World News

Every October in Canada, there's a very special boat race. It was invented in 1999 by a local boy, Danny Dill. He got the idea because his father grew giant pumpkins. The Giant Pumpkin Boat Race takes around 20 minutes from start to finish, and the course is 800 meters long. Now, let's learn how to enjoy the race. First, you need a good pumpkin. ( ① ) It has to be very big, around 250 kg, because you need to sit inside it. ( ② ) Round boats are too hard to control. ( ③ ) When you get the right one, next you have to cut off its top and remove all the flesh. ( ④ ) It's hard work. ( ⑤ ) Can you fit inside it? Good. Now, all you need is a paddle and a lot of strength! Are you ready? Go! Paddle as hard as you can! Try to stay afloat!

| | | |
|---|---|---|
| invent v. ______ | local a. ______ | grow v. ______ |
| giant a. ______ | pumpkin n. ______ | take v. ______ |
| inside prep. ______ | rounded a. ______ | control v. ______ |
| cut off ______ | remove v. ______ | flesh n. ______ |
| fit v. ______ | paddle n. ______ v. ______ | strength n. ______ |
| afloat a. ______ | | |

**1** The Giant Pumpkin Boat Race에 관한 윗글의 내용과 일치하지 않는 것은?

① 호박을 재배하는 아버지를 둔 소년이 만든 대회이다.

② 경기에 소요되는 시간은 약 20분이다.

③ 경기가 벌어지는 코스의 길이는 800미터이다.

④ 경기에 참가하려면 호박을 직접 재배해야 한다.

⑤ 경기에 사용되는 호박은 약 250킬로그램이다.

**2** 글의 흐름으로 보아 주어진 문장이 들어갈 위치로 가장 알맞은 것은?

And it shouldn't be too rounded, like a ball.

① ② ③ ④ ⑤

서술형

**3** 윗글에서 The Giant Pumpkin Boat race에 둥근 호박이 적합하지 않은 이유를 찾아 영어로 쓰시오.

___

**이탈리아의 오렌지 전투**

이탈리아 북부의 작은 도시 이브레아는 주민수가 2만명 남짓 되는 작은 도시이다. 하지만 이 작은 도시에 매년 3월이면 10만 명이 넘는 관광객들이 찾아온다. 바로 사흘간 진행되는 오렌지 전투 때문이다. 이 전투는 중세시대, 난폭한 영주에게 시민들이 저항했던 사건을 계기로 시작되었다고 한다. 참가자들은 여러 개의 시민팀과 마차팀으로 나뉘어 서로에게 사정없이 오렌지를 던지는데, 빨간 모자를 쓰고 있는 관중에게는 절대로 오렌지를 던져서는 안 된다. 전투가 끝나면 거리는 터진 오렌지로 산을 이루게 되는데, 전투기간 동안 쓰이는 오렌지의 양이 무려 700여 톤이나 된다고 한다. 이 전투가 끝나면 군중 속에 숨어 있던 심판이 가장 잘 싸운 팀을 선정하여 상을 준다.

Information

Beware of the invisible enemy! Think back to when you last left the bathroom. Now, is your toilet lid open? Or is it closed? You don't even remember, do you? Then, from now on, you'd better pay attention to where the lid is. Dr. Charles Gerba of the University of Arizona recently studied hundreds of toilets in private homes and public places. He used special cameras to take pictures of toilets flushing. The slow-motion pictures showed exactly what happens when a toilet is flushed. "You can't see it with your eyes, but it's like a bomb exploding," said Dr. Gerba. Tiny drops of dirty water and millions of germs spray far and wide. The dirty water and tiny germs go everywhere. So, make sure that you keep your bathroom very clean. To be really safe, always close the toilet lid ________________________!

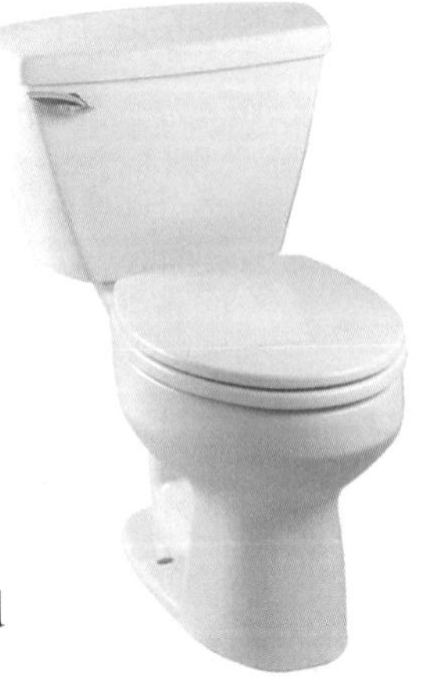

| | | |
|---|---|---|
| beware of v. ________ | invisible a. ________ | think back to ________ |
| last ad. ________ | toilet n. ________ | lid n. ________ |
| from now on ________ | had better ________ | pay attention to ________ |
| recently ad. ________ | hundreds of ________ | private a. ________ |
| public place ________ | flush v. ________ | slow-motion a. ________ |
| bomb n. ________ | explode v. ________ | tiny a. ________ |
| drop n. ________ | millions of ________ | germ n. ________ |
| spray v. ________ | far and wide ________ | make sure ________ |
| supply n. ________ | | |

**1** 윗글의 제목으로 가장 알맞은 것은?

① How to Clean the Toilet
② What Makes Your Toilet Explode
③ The Best Cleaning Supplies for You
④ Why You Should Close Your Toilet Lid
⑤ Different Kinds of Germs in Your Toilet

**2** 윗글의 빈칸에 들어갈 말로 가장 알맞은 것은?

① before you flush
② before you turn off the light
③ before you leave the toilet
④ after you wash your hands
⑤ when you walk into the toilet

서술형

**3** 윗글에서 밑줄 친 Tiny drops of dirty water and millions of germs spray far and wide.를 비유한 표현을 찾아 세 단어의 영어로 쓰시오.

______________________________

이미지 맵 글을 읽고, 빈칸을 완성하시오.

**Title:**
(1)____________
____________

A doctor studied many (2)__________ in private homes and public places.

He used special cameras to see what happens when a toilet is (3)__________.

The dirty water and tiny germs go (4)__________.

You should (5)__________ the toilet lid when you flush.

# Review Test

## 1 Art

**A** 다음 중 단어의 정의가 잘못된 것은?

① cool: being fashionable or attractive
② dusty: free from dirt or unwanted marks
③ draw: to produce a picture using a pencil
④ work: the total output of a writer or artist
⑤ park: to put a car in a particular place for a period of time

**B** 우리말과 일치하도록 〈보기〉에서 단어를 골라 문장을 완성하시오.

보기 paint left without appear

1 Humans can't live ____________ water and air. 인간은 물과 공기 없이 살 수 없다.
2 My sister spilt red ____________ on my picture. 여동생이 내 그림 위에 빨간 물감을 쏟았다.
3 After 30 seconds, the actor will ____________ on the screen.
30초 후에 그 배우가 화면에 등장할 것이다.
4 I ____________ my keys on the table this morning, but now they aren't there.
나는 오늘 아침에 탁자 위에 열쇠를 두었는데 지금은 열쇠가 거기에 없다.

## 2 Humor

**A** 밑줄 친 단어와 반대되는 의미의 단어를 고르시오.

1 All of us agree to keep the rule in the library.
① allow ② reject ③ admit ④ approve ⑤ follow

2 Today, your English class will begin one hour ahead.
① before ② earlier ③ advanced ④ previously ⑤ behind

**B** 우리말과 일치하도록 〈보기〉에서 단어를 골라 문장을 완성하시오.

보기 plan reach by mistake type

1 Matthew dropped his cup ____________. Matthew는 실수로 컵을 떨어뜨렸다.
2 We ____________ to open a new store at a mall. 우리는 쇼핑몰에 새 가게를 열 계획이다.
3 I'm looking for someone who can ____________ the tax report.
나는 세금 보고서를 입력할 수 있는 사람을 찾고 있다.
4 Hurry up or we won't ____________ the airport on time.
서둘러 그렇지 않으면 우리는 제시간에 공항에 도착할 수 없을 거야.

## 3 World News

**A** 〈보기〉의 밑줄 친 around와 같은 의미로 쓰인 것은?

보기 It has to be very big, around 250 kg.

① They walked around the lake.

② The earth moves around the sun.

③ I found an old box around my garden.

④ The post office is just around the corner.

⑤ It takes around 30 minutes to fix the car.

**B** 우리말과 일치하도록 〈보기〉에서 단어를 골라 문장을 완성하시오.

보기 control inside remove afloat

1 Jack, ____________ your cap from the table. Jack, 탁자 위에 있는 네 모자를 치워라.

2 Sharks must move around to keep ____________. 상어는 물에 떠있기 위해 움직여야 한다.

3 You should learn how to ____________ your anger. 당신은 화를 조절하는 방법을 배워야 한다.

4 It started to rain, so we had to go ____________ the house.
비가 내리기 시작해서 우리는 집 안으로 들어가야 했다.

## 4 Information

**A** 밑줄 친 단어와 비슷한 의미의 단어를 고르시오.

1 Beware of pickpockets in Rome.
① ignore ② invite ③ take over ④ watch out ⑤ face

2 Do you want my private email address?
① personal ② common ③ known ④ principal ⑤ public

**B** 우리말과 일치하도록 〈보기〉에서 단어를 골라 문장을 완성하시오.

보기 from now on explodes had better far and wide

1 I think you ____________ go to the party. 내 생각에 너는 그 파티에 가는 게 좋겠어.

2 The dangerous germs can spread ____________. 그 위험한 세균이 사방팔방으로 퍼질 수 있다.

3 You should lie face down when a bomb ____________. 폭탄이 폭발하면 땅에 엎드려야 한다.

4 Don't bring any beverage into the classroom ____________.
지금부터 어떤 음료도 교실 안으로 가지고 오지 마라.

# 어휘 재충전

## 1 Art

- □ unusual a. 특이한, 흔치 않은
- □ create v. 만들어 내다
- □ without prep. ~ 없이
- □ paint n. 물감
- □ brush n. 붓
- □ work n. 작품, 일
- □ dust n. 먼지
- □ appear v. 나타나다
- □ leave v. ~을 두고 가다
- □ dusty a. 먼지투성이인
- □ car park 주차장
- □ parking fee 주차 요금

## 2 Humor

- □ plan v. 계획하다
- □ agree v. 동의하다
- □ ahead ad. 먼저, 앞서서
- □ quick a. 빠른, 신속한
- □ key n. (키보드의) 키
- □ by mistake 실수로, 잘못해서
- □ type v. 입력하다
- □ reach v. 도착하다
- □ instead ad. 대신에
- □ preacher n. 설교가, 목사
- □ kind n. 종류, ~한 부류의 사람
- □ preach v. 설교하다
- □ hell n. 지옥
- □ the day before 그 전날
- □ widow n. 미망인, 과부

## 3 World News

- □ invent v. 창안하다, 고안하다
- □ local a. 지역의, 현지의
- □ grow v. 재배하다, 기르다
- □ giant a. 거대한
- □ pumpkin n. 호박
- □ take v. ~이 걸리다
- □ inside prep. ~의 안에
- □ rounded a. 둥근
- □ control v. 조작하다, 조절하다
- □ cut off 잘라내다
- □ remove v. 제거하다
- □ flesh n. 살, 고기, 과육
- □ fit v. (~에 들어가기에) 알맞다
- □ paddle n. 노 v. 노를 젓다
- □ strength n. 힘
- □ afloat a. 물 위에 떠서

## 4 Information

- □ beware of v. ~을 조심하다
- □ invisible a. 보이지 않는
- □ think back to ~을 회상하다
- □ last ad. 최근에
- □ toilet n. 화장실, 변기
- □ lid n. 뚜껑
- □ from now on 지금부터
- □ had better ~하는 것이 좋다
- □ pay attention to ~에 주의를 기울이다
- □ recently ad. 최근에
- □ hundreds of 수백의
- □ private a. 개인의
- □ public place 공공장소
- □ flush v. (변기의) 물을 내리다
- □ slow-motion a. 느린 동작의, 슬로모션의
- □ bomb n. 폭탄
- □ explode v. 폭발하다
- □ tiny a. 아주 작은, 미세한
- □ drop n. 방울
- □ millions of 수백만의
- □ germ n. 세균
- □ spray v. 뿌려지다
- □ far and wide 사방팔방으로
- □ make sure 반드시 ~하다
- □ supply n. 용품, 공급

Memo

Memo

Memo

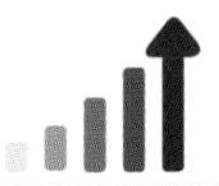

NEXUS Edu

# LEVEL CHART

| | 초1 | 초2 | 초3 | 초4 | 초5 | 초6 | 중1 | 중2 | 중3 | 고1 | 고2 | 고3 |
|---|---|---|---|---|---|---|---|---|---|---|---|---|
| VOCA | 초등필수 영단어 1-2 · 3-4 · 5-6학년용 | | | | | | | | | | | |
| VOCA | | | | | The VOCA + (플러스) 1~7 | | | | | | | |
| VOCA | | | THIS IS VOCABULARY 입문 · 초급 · 중급 | | | | | 고급 · 어원 · 수능 완성 · 뉴텝스 | | | | |
| VOCA | | | | | | | WORD FOCUS 중등 종합 5000 · 고등 필수 5000 · 고등 종합 9500 | | | | | |
| Grammar | | | 초등필수 영문법 + 쓰기 1~2 | | | | | | | | | |
| Grammar | | | OK Grammar 1~4 | | | | | | | | | |
| Grammar | | | This Is Grammar Starter 1~3 | | | | | | | | | |
| Grammar | | | | | This Is Grammar 초급~고급 (각 2권: 총 6권) | | | | | | | |
| Grammar | | | | | | Grammar 공감 1~3 | | | | | | |
| Grammar | | | | | | Grammar 101 1~3 | | | | | | |
| Grammar | | | | | | Grammar Bridge 1~3 | | | | | | |
| Grammar | | | | | | 중학영문법 뽀개기 1~3 | | | | | | |
| Grammar | | | | | | The Grammar Starter, 1~3 | | | | | | |
| Grammar | | | | | | | | 구사일생 (구문독해 Basic) 1~2 | | | | |
| Grammar | | | | | | | | | 구문독해 204 1~2 | | | |
| Grammar | | | | | | | | 그래머 캡처 1~2 | | | | |
| Grammar | | | | | | | | | [특급 단기 특강] 어법어휘 모의고사 | | | |

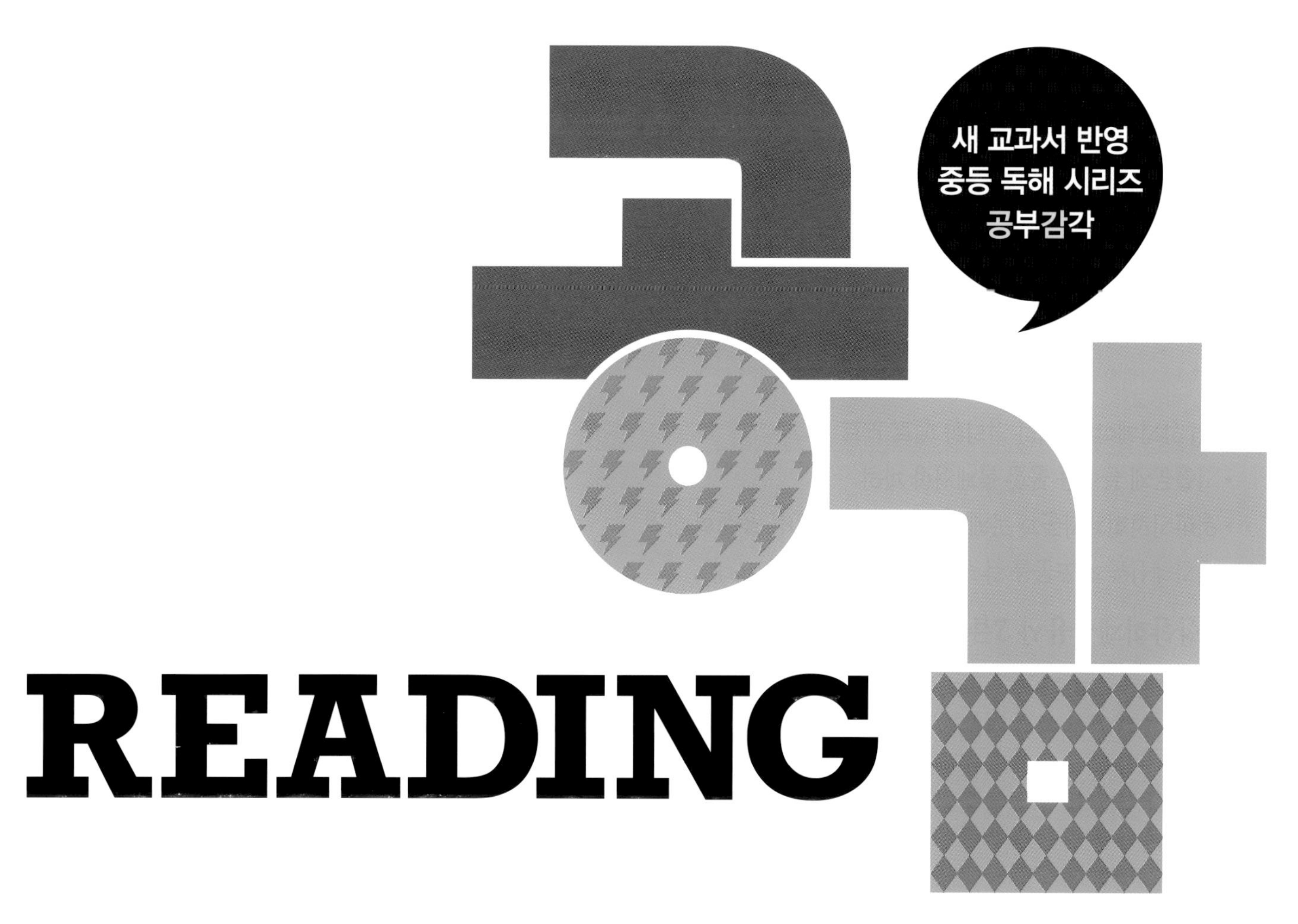


넥서스영어교육연구소 지음

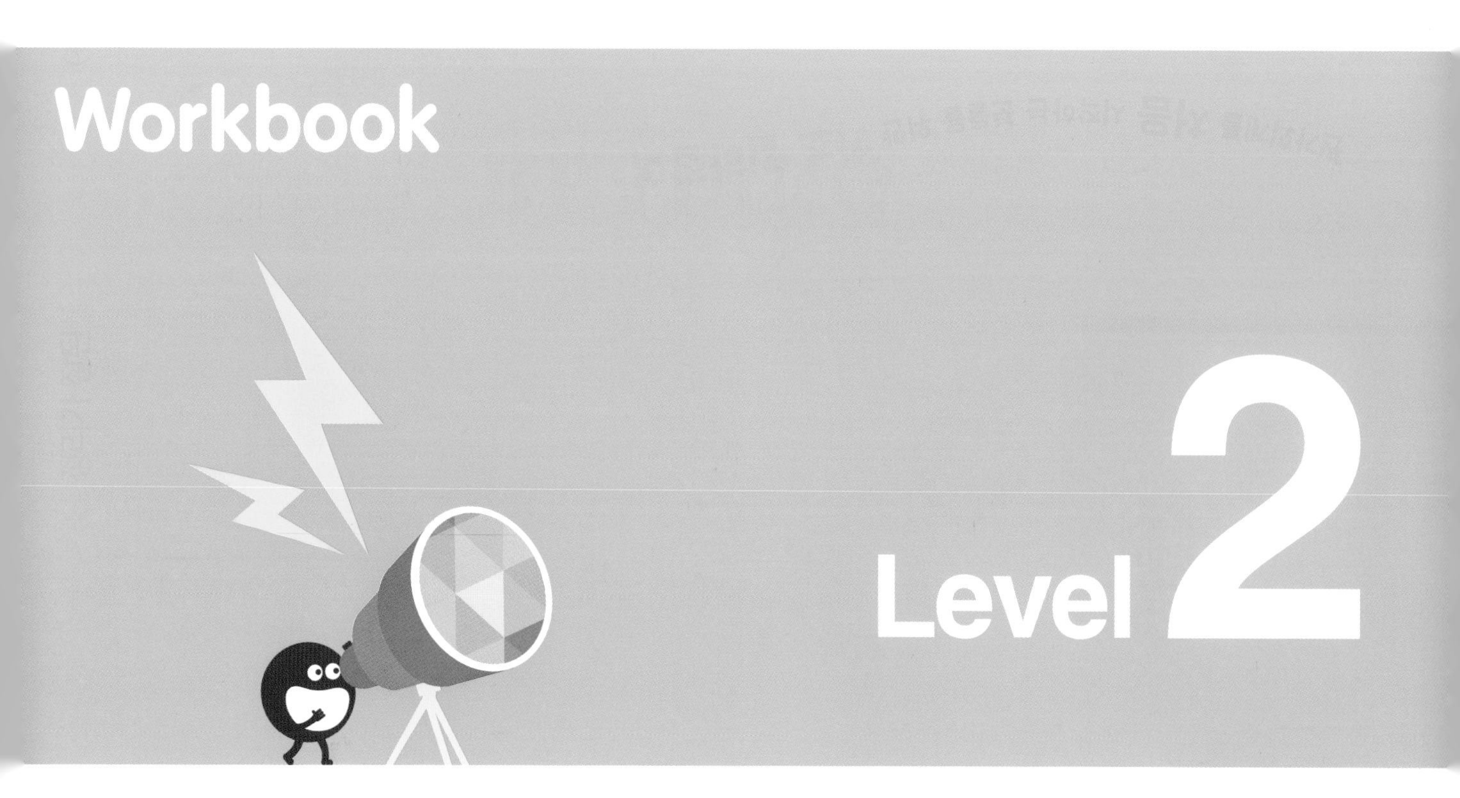


NEXUS Edu

# 1 Origin

Chapter 1

**A** 영어는 우리말로, 우리말은 영어로 쓰시오.

1 mistake ____________

2 prepare ____________

3 melt ____________

4 remain ____________

5 serve ____________

6 ~이 떨어지다 ____________

7 굽다 ____________

8 결정하다 ____________

9 덩어리 ____________

10 맛있는 ____________

**B** 〈보기〉와 같이 우리말과 같은 뜻이 되도록 문장을 완성하시오.

보기 Ruth는 초콜릿바를 사용하기로 결심했다. (use, pieces of, a chocolate candy bar)
→ Ruth decided to use pieces of a chocolate candy bar.

1 Jennifer는 그에게 진실을 말하기로 결심했다. (tell, him, the truth)
→ ____________

2 그녀는 외국에서 공부하기로 결심했다. (study, abroad)
→ ____________

3 나는 그 빨간 신발을 사기로 결정했다. (buy, the red shoes)
→ ____________

**C** 우리말과 같은 뜻이 되도록 주어진 단어를 배열하여 문장을 완성하시오.

1 그녀는 코코아가루가 다 떨어졌다. (cocoa powder, she, was out of)
→ ____________

2 그녀는 초콜릿 조각이 녹을 것이라고 예상했다. (would melt, she, the chocolate pieces, expected)
→ ____________

3 초콜릿 조각은 전혀 녹지 않았다. (at all, the chocolate pieces, weren't melted)
→ ____________

# 2 Humor

Chapter 1

## A 영어는 우리말로, 우리말은 영어로 쓰시오.

1 trail ____________

2 come out of ____________

3 chase ____________

4 climb up ____________

5 backpack ____________

6 입다, 신다 ____________

7 ~일 거라고 생각하다 ____________

8 ~에 접근하다 ____________

9 뛰어내리다 ____________

10 ~보다 더 빨리 달리다 ____________

## B 〈보기〉와 같이 우리말과 같은 뜻이 되도록 문장을 완성하시오.

보기 나는 곰보다 더 빨리 달릴 필요가 없다. (outrun, the bear)
→ I don't have to outrun the bear.

1 너는 천천히 말할 필요가 없다. (speak, slowly)
→ ____________

2 우리는 내일까지 이 일을 끝낼 필요가 없다. (finish, this work, by tomorrow)
→ ____________

3 그들은 그 실수에 대해 사과할 필요가 없다. (apologize for, the mistake)
→ ____________

## C 우리말과 같은 뜻이 되도록 주어진 단어를 배열하여 문장을 완성하시오.

1 곰 한 마리가 도보 여행자들을 뒤쫓기 시작한다. (the hikers, a bear, chasing, starts)
→ ____________

2 그는 자신의 배낭에서 운동화를 꺼낸다. (gets, he, out of his backpack, his sneakers)
→ ____________

3 우리는 필사적으로 도망칠 거야. (run for, we'll, our lives)
→ ____________

# 3 World News

**A** 영어는 우리말로, 우리말은 영어로 쓰시오.

1 silent ____________
2 ban ____________
3 calm down ____________
4 except for ____________
5 serve ____________
6 가치, 진가 ____________
7 절, 사찰 ____________
8 명상 ____________
9 식욕 ____________
10 향상시키다, 개선하다 ____________

**B** 〈보기〉와 같이 우리말과 같은 뜻이 되도록 문장을 완성하시오.

보기 명상은 우리의 신체뿐만 아니라 우리의 마음도 갈고 닦게 해 준다.
(meditation, could, sharpen, our bodies, our minds)
→ Meditation could sharpen our minds as well as our bodies.

1 그 신발은 예쁠 뿐만 아니라 실용적이다. (the shoes, are, pretty, useful)
→ ____________

2 그는 작가뿐만 아니라 감독으로도 활동했다. (he, worked as, a writer, a director)
→ ____________

3 그녀는 음식을 먹는 것뿐만 아니라 요리하는 것도 좋아한다. (she, likes, eating food, cooking)
→ ____________

**C** 우리말과 같은 뜻이 되도록 주어진 단어를 배열하여 문장을 완성하시오.

1 사람들이 식당에서 하고 싶어 하는 것은 무엇인가? (in restaurants, do, people, what, to do, like)
→ ____________

2 나는 사찰에서 아이디어를 얻었다. (from a Buddhist temple, got, I, the idea)
→ ____________

3 침묵의 아침 식사는 급한 내 마음을 차분하게 해 준다. (my busy mind, silent breakfast, calms down)
→ ____________

# 4 Stories

Chapter 1

**A** 영어는 우리말로, 우리말은 영어로 쓰시오.

1 alive ______________
2 all of a sudden ______________
3 media ______________
4 be disappointed by ______________
5 land on ______________
6 주차하다 ______________
7 기적 ______________
8 대답, 응답 ______________
9 발생하다 ______________
10 (붙)들고 있다 ______________

**B** 〈보기〉와 같이 우리말과 같은 뜻이 되도록 문장을 완성하시오.

> 보기 그는 그 답변에 실망했다. (the response)
> → He was disappointed by the response.

1 Lucy는 자신의 과학 시험 점수에 실망했다. (her science score)
→ ______________

2 우리는 축구 경기 결과에 실망했다. (the result of the soccer game)
→ ______________

3 나는 그녀의 말에 실망했다. (her words)
→ ______________

**C** 우리말과 같은 뜻이 되도록 주어진 단어를 배열하여 문장을 완성하시오.

1 그는 신선한 물이 든 통 안에 물고기를 넣었다. (the fish, in a bowl, of fresh water, put, he)
→ ______________

2 그 남자는 그 기적적인 일을 알리기 위해 언론사에 전화를 걸었다.
(called, the miracle, the man, to report, the media)
→ ______________

3 펠리칸이 입에 무엇을 물고 있는지 보아라. (hold, what, see, in their mouth, pelicans)
→ ______________

# 1 Food

Chapter 2

**A** 영어는 우리말로, 우리말은 영어로 쓰시오.

1 terrible ______________
2 line up ______________
3 stand ______________
4 spicy ______________
5 badly ______________
6 적시다, 담그다 ______________
7 조리법 ______________
8 악취를 풍기다 ______________
9 바삭한 ______________
10 감추다, 숨다 ______________

**B** 〈보기〉와 같이 우리말과 같은 뜻이 되도록 문장을 완성하시오.

보기 누구도 감출 수 없는 것은 그 지독한 냄새이다. (nobody, can, hide, be, the terrible smell)
→ What nobody can hide is the terrible smell.

1 내가 좋아하는 것은 갈색 스카프이다. (I, like, be, the brown scarf)
→ ______________________________

2 우리 아빠가 내게 준 것은 새 자전거였다. (my dad, gave, me, be, a new bicycle)
→ ______________________________

3 그가 자신의 가방에 넣은 것은 자였다. (he, put, in his bag, be, a ruler)
→ ______________________________

**C** 우리말과 같은 뜻이 되도록 주어진 단어를 배열하여 문장을 완성하시오.

1 이것은 세계에서 가장 맛있는 음식 중 하나이다. (one of, this, most delicious foods, is, the world's)
→ ______________________________

2 사람들이 취두부 가판대에 줄을 서 있다. (line up, people, at stinky tofu stands)
→ ______________________________

3 두부가 노릇노릇하고 바삭할 때까지 바짝 튀겨진다. (deep fried, tofu, is, until it's, golden and crispy)
→ ______________________________

# 2 Culture

Chapter 2

**A** 영어는 우리말로, 우리말은 영어로 쓰시오.

1 vending machine ____________
2 nearly ____________
3 far away ____________
4 yummy ____________
5 invention ____________
6 심지어 ____________
7 ~의 안에 ____________
8 수요 ____________
9 상상하다 ____________
10 자신의 ____________

**B** 〈보기〉와 같이 우리말과 같은 뜻이 되도록 문장을 완성하시오.

보기 당신 자신의 자동판매기를 만들 수 있다고 상상해 봐라. (can, make, your own, vending machine)
→ Imagine that you can make your own vending machine.

1 네가 하늘을 날 수 있다고 상상해 봐라. (can, fly, in the sky)
→ ____________

2 네가 금메달을 딴다고 생각해 봐라. (win, the gold medal)
→ ____________

3 네가 로봇 요리사를 가지고 있다고 생각해 봐라. (have, a robot chef)
→ ____________

**C** 우리말과 같은 뜻이 되도록 주어진 단어를 배열하여 문장을 완성하시오.

1 자동판매기는 뜨거운 커피보다 훨씬 많은 것을 팔 수 있다.
(can, vending machines, sell, hot coffee, much more than)
→ ____________

2 상추는 기계 안에서 자란다. (grow, lettuce plants, inside the machine)
→ ____________

3 사람들은 새로운 자동판매기를 계속 개발한다. (people, new vending machines, inventing, keep)
→ ____________

# 3 Life

Chapter 2

**A** 영어는 우리말로, 우리말은 영어로 쓰시오.

1 happen ______________

2 turn ______________

3 a bit of ______________

4 object ______________

5 hollow ______________

6 지하실 ______________

7 조언 ______________

8 살아남다 ______________

9 움켜잡다 ______________

10 엎드리다 ______________

**B** 〈보기〉와 같이 우리말과 같은 뜻이 되도록 문장을 완성하시오.

보기 너는 토네이도 경고음을 듣자마자, 곧장 지하실로 가라.
(hear, a tornado warning sound, go straight, to your basement)
→ As soon as you hear a tornado warning sound, go straight to your basement.

1 너는 일어나자마자, 나에게 이메일을 보내라. (wake up, send, me, an email)
→ ______________

2 너는 집에 오자마자, 불을 켜라. (get home, turn on, the light)
→ ______________

3 너는 학교에 가자마자, 보고서를 제출해라. (go to school, hand in, the report)
→ ______________

**C** 우리말과 같은 뜻이 되도록 주어진 단어를 배열하여 문장을 완성하시오.

1 깨진 유리는 가장 큰 사망의 원인이다. (is, broken glass, the biggest killer)
→ ______________

2 당신의 머리를 덮을 담요나 베개를 움켜잡아라. (blankets or pillows, to cover, grab, your head)
→ ______________

3 그것은 당신이 빨려 드는 것으로부터 구해 줄지도 모른다. (might, save, it, from being sucked up, you)
→ ______________

# 4 Opinion

**A** 영어는 우리말로, 우리말은 영어로 쓰시오.

1 ask ______________
2 hang out with ______________
3 find out ______________
4 lie ______________
5 make a mistake ______________
6 문자메시지를 보내다 ______________
7 심지어, ~도 ______________
8 다치게 하다 ______________
9 한 번 ______________
10 ~와 절교하다 ______________

**B** 〈보기〉와 같이 우리말과 같은 뜻이 되도록 문장을 완성하시오.

보기 만약에 그가 너의 기분을 상하게 하고 싶지 않았다면 어떻게 하지? (didn't want, to hurt, your feelings)
→ What if he didn't want to hurt your feelings?

1 만약에 내가 틀렸다면 어떻게 하지? (was, wrong)
→ ______________

2 만약에 네가 외계인과 대화할 수 있다면 어떨까? (can, communicate with, aliens)
→ ______________

3 만약에 우리가 엄청난 보너스를 받는다면 어떨까? (get, a big bonus)
→ ______________

**C** 우리말과 같은 뜻이 되도록 주어진 단어를 배열하여 문장을 완성하시오.

1 좋은 친구가 정말 중요하다. (good friends, very important, are)
→ ______________

2 그는 다른 친구들과 놀고 있었다. (he, other friends, was hanging out with)
→ ______________

3 친한 친구는 서로에게 거짓말을 해서는 안 된다. (best friends, each other, lie to, shouldn't)
→ ______________

# 1 Psychology

Chapter 3

**A** 영어는 우리말로, 우리말은 영어로 쓰시오.

1 stressed ____________

2 settle down ____________

3 have an effect on ____________

4 moment ____________

5 imagination ____________

6 방법 ____________

7 중요하다 ____________

8 없애주다, 줄이다 ____________

9 작가 ____________

10 ~에 의하면 ____________

**B** 〈보기〉와 같이 우리말과 같은 뜻이 되도록 문장을 완성하시오.

보기 책을 읽는 것은 다른 방법보다 효과가 더 빠르다. (reading, works, fast, other methods)
→ Reading works faster than other methods.

1 그녀는 우리 중 누구보다 열심히 일한다. (she, works, hard, any of us)
→ ____________

2 그 공연은 우리가 기대했던 것보다 좋았다. (the show, was, good, we, expected)
→ ____________

3 이 꽃은 다른 식물보다 더 느리게 자란다. (this flower, is growing, slow, the other plants)
→ ____________

**C** 우리말과 같은 뜻이 되도록 주어진 단어를 배열하여 문장을 완성하시오.

1 독서가 스트레스를 푸는 가장 좋은 방법이다. (the best way, is, reading, to relieve stress)
→ ____________

2 당신이 무슨 책을 읽는지는 중요하지 않다. (matter, what book, read, doesn't, it, you)
→ ____________

3 너는 작가의 상상력을 즐길 수 있다. (can, the author's imagination, you, enjoy)
→ ____________

# 2 Stories

**A** 영어는 우리말로, 우리말은 영어로 쓰시오.

1 collect ______________
2 garbage ______________
3 donation ______________
4 self-esteem ______________
5 success ______________
6 소유물, 소지품 ______________
7 자존감 ______________
8 나누어 주다 ______________
9 적절한, 제대로 된 ______________
10 보여주다, 제시하다 ______________

**B** <보기>와 같이 우리말과 같은 뜻이 되도록 문장을 완성하시오.

> **보기** 그녀는 가능한 한 빨리 그것들을 나누어 주었다. (gave, them, away, quickly)
> → She gave them away as quickly as she could.

1 그녀는 가능한 한 크게 비명을 질렀다. (cried out, loudly)
→ ______________________________

2 그는 할 수 있는 한 많이 먹었다. (ate, much)
→ ______________________________

3 Daniel은 가능한 한 열심히 공부했다. (studied, hard)
→ ______________________________

**C** 우리말과 같은 뜻이 되도록 주어진 단어를 배열하여 문장을 완성하시오.

1 그녀는 약 2,300개의 짐 가방을 모았다. (collected, luggage, about 2,300 pieces of, she)
→ ______________________________

2 그 아이들은 제대로 된 가방을 가질 수 있었다. (the children, luggage, proper, have, could)
→ ______________________________

3 그녀는 자신의 의견을 시민 단체에 내 놓았다. (presented, her ideas, she, to civic groups)
→ ______________________________

# 3 World News

Chapter 3

**A** 영어는 우리말로, 우리말은 영어로 쓰시오.

1 crime ______________

2 arrest ______________

3 ancient ______________

4 seller ______________

5 belong to ______________

6 특이한, 흔치 않은 ______________

7 죽은 ______________

8 재산 ______________

9 국왕의 ______________

10 꼬리 ______________

**B** 〈보기〉와 같이 우리말과 같은 뜻이 되도록 문장을 완성하시오.

보기 그들은 그가 너무 어렸기 때문에 체포하지 않았다. (didn't, arrest, him, young)
→ They didn't arrest him because he was too young.

1 그는 너무 어렸기 때문에 운전을 할 수 없었다. (couldn't, drive, young)
→ ______________

2 그녀는 너무 피곤했기 때문에 저녁을 요리할 수 없었다. (couldn't, cook, dinner, tired)
→ ______________

3 나는 너무 바빴기 때문에 영화를 보러 갈 수 없었다. (couldn't, go to the movies, busy)
→ ______________

**C** 우리말과 같은 뜻이 되도록 주어진 단어를 배열하여 문장을 완성하시오.

1 고래가 온라인상에서 판매 중이었다. (were, whales, for sale online)
→ ______________

2 특이한 범죄가 영국 경찰에 보고되었다. (was reported to, an unusual crime, U.K. police)
→ ______________

3 고래의 머리는 왕실의 권력을 상징한다. (a symbol of, a whale's heads, royal power, was)
→ ______________

# 4 Information

Chapter 3

**A** 영어는 우리말로, 우리말은 영어로 쓰시오.

1 tourist ____________

2 historic ____________

3 expensive ____________

4 passenger ____________

5 public transportation ____________

6 독특한, 특별한 ____________

7 허락하다 ____________

8 마차 ____________

9 오염, 공해 ____________

10 노를 젓다 ____________

**B** 〈보기〉와 같이 우리말과 같은 뜻이 되도록 문장을 완성하시오.

> **보기** 당신은 어떤 종류의 대중교통을 이용합니까? (public transportation, use)
> → What kinds of public transportation do you use?

1 당신은 어떤 종류의 음식을 좋아합니까? (foods, like)

→ ____________

2 당신은 어떤 종류의 물건이 필요합니까? (items, need)

→ ____________

3 그들은 어떤 종류의 방을 원합니까? (rooms, want)

→ ____________

**C** 우리말과 같은 뜻이 되도록 주어진 단어를 배열하여 문장을 완성하시오.

1 여기 몇 가지 독특한 대중교통 수단이 있다. (some, public transportation, here, unique forms of, are)

→ ____________

2 자전거 택시는 암스테르담을 여행하기에 완벽한 수단이다.
(the perfect way, bike taxis, are, Amsterdam, to tour)

→ ____________

3 당신은 40분에 135달러를 지불해야 한다. (have to, $135, for 40 minutes, you, pay)

→ ____________

# 1 Humor

Chapter 4

**A** 영어는 우리말로, 우리말은 영어로 쓰시오.

1 scholar ______________
2 be proud of ______________
3 biology ______________
4 thanks to ______________
5 all of a sudden ______________
6 소리치다 ______________
7 ~이 부족한 ______________
8 교육 ______________
9 가라앉다 ______________
10 지식 ______________

**B** 〈보기〉와 같이 우리말과 같은 뜻이 되도록 문장을 완성하시오.

보기 그 배가 가라앉기 시작했다. (the boat, sink)
→ The boat began to sink.

1 Judy는 영어 공부를 하기 시작했다. (Judy, study, English)
→ ______________

2 그들은 크게 웃기 시작했다. (they, laugh, loudly)
→ ______________

3 그녀는 울기 시작했다. (she, cry)
→ ______________

**C** 우리말과 같은 뜻이 되도록 주어진 단어를 배열하여 문장을 완성하시오.

1 한 학자가 낚시 여행을 갔다. (was, a fishing trip, a scholar, on)
→ ______________

2 그는 자신의 지식에 매우 자부심을 느꼈다. (his knowledge, was, very proud of, he)
→ ______________

3 당신은 교육 부족으로 죽게 될 겁니다! (your lack of, you'll, education, die from)
→ ______________

# 2 Technology

Chapter 4

**A** 영어는 우리말로, 우리말은 영어로 쓰시오.

1 wheel ______________

2 folding ______________

3 develop ______________

4 luggage ______________

5 signal ______________

6 추적하다, 뒤쫓다 ______________

7 ~할 수 있게 하다 ______________

8 뒤에 ______________

9 위험을 알리다 ______________

10 ~을 따라잡다, 뒤지지 않다 ______________

**B** 〈보기〉와 같이 우리말과 같은 뜻이 되도록 문장을 완성하시오.

> 보기 공항에서 가방을 잃어버린 적이 있습니까? (lose, a bag, at the airport)
> → Have you ever lost a bag at the airport?

1 그의 명곡을 들어본 적이 있습니까? (hear, his famous song)

→ ______________________________

2 뉴욕에 가본 적이 있습니까? (be, to New York)

→ ______________________________

3 새로 이사 온 이웃 사람과 이야기해 본 적이 있습니까? (talk to, a new neighbor)

→ ______________________________

**C** 우리말과 같은 뜻이 되도록 주어진 단어를 배열하여 문장을 완성하시오.

1 그 가방은 당신이 어디로 가든지 당신을 따라간다. (you, the bag, wherever, follows, go, you)

→ ______________________________

2 그 신호는 Hop이 당신을 따라갈 수 있게 해 준다. (enable, you, the signals, to follow, Hop)

→ ______________________________

3 발명가들은 더 빠른 모델을 개발하는 중이다. (are developing, a faster model, the inventors)

→ ______________________________

# 3 Information

Chapter 4

**A** 영어는 우리말로, 우리말은 영어로 쓰시오.

1 method ______________
2 recommend ______________
3 itchy ______________
4 odor ______________
5 calm ______________
6 제거하다 ______________
7 뿌리다 ______________
8 방울 ______________
9 예민한, 민감한 ______________
10 없애주다, 덜어주다 ______________

**B** 〈보기〉와 같이 우리말과 같은 뜻이 되도록 문장을 완성하시오.

보기 에센셜 오일은 사람들의 행복감을 높여주는 데 사용된다.
(essential oils, improve, people's feelings of well-being)
→ Essential oils are used to improve people's feelings of well-being.

1 그 소프트웨어는 너의 컴퓨터를 고치는 데 사용된다. (the software, fix, your computer)
→ ______________

2 이 약은 고통을 줄이는 데 사용된다. (this pill, reduce, pain)
→ ______________

3 그 지우개는 벽의 얼룩을 지우는 데 사용된다. (the eraser, remove, spots, on the wall)
→ ______________

**C** 우리말과 같은 뜻이 되도록 주어진 단어를 배열하여 문장을 완성하시오.

1 여기 애완동물을 위한 몇 가지 훌륭한 에센셜 오일이 있다. (several good essential oils, are, for pets, here)
→ ______________

2 라벤더 에센셜 오일은 냄새를 제거해 줄 것이다. (will remove, lavender essential oil, odors)
→ ______________

3 개들은 종종 피부 가려움증이 생긴다. (often, itchy skin, get, dogs)
→ ______________

# 4 Stories

Chapter 4

**A** 영어는 우리말로, 우리말은 영어로 쓰시오.

1 respond to ____________
2 emergency ____________
3 bite ____________
4 take out ____________
5 prepare ____________
6 즉시 ____________
7 주의 깊게 살펴보다 ____________
8 버릇없는, 말썽꾸러기의 ____________
9 훔치다 ____________
10 울타리 ____________

**B** 〈보기〉와 같이 우리말과 같은 뜻이 되도록 문장을 완성하시오.

보기 그의 걸작은 돌만큼 단단하다. (his masterpiece, hard, a rock)
→ His masterpiece is as hard as a rock.

1 그는 자신의 아버지만큼 키가 크다. (he, tall, his father)
→ ____________

2 이 음료수는 꿀만큼 달다. (this drink, sweet, honey)
→ ____________

3 과정은 결과만큼 중요하다. (the process, important, the result)
→ ____________

**C** 우리말과 같은 뜻이 되도록 주어진 단어를 배열하여 문장을 완성하시오.

1 두 명의 경찰관은 가능한 한 빨리 그곳으로 운전해 갔다.
(drove there, two police officers, they could, as fast as)
→ ____________

2 한 남자가 집에서 달려나왔다. (a man, running out of, came, the house)
→ ____________

3 그 경찰관들은 자세히 살펴보기 위해 다가갔다. (to take a close look, the police officers, walked over)
→ ____________

# 1 Body

Chapter 5

**A** 영어는 우리말로, 우리말은 영어로 쓰시오.

1 hormone ____________
2 harsh ____________
3 squeeze ____________
4 infection ____________
5 treatment ____________
6 여드름 ____________
7 십대의 ____________
8 활발한 ____________
9 방지하다, 피하다 ____________
10 전문적인 ____________

**B** 〈보기〉와 같이 우리말과 같은 뜻이 되도록 문장을 완성하시오.

> 보기 여기 피부과 의사의 몇 가지 조언이 있다. (some advice, from skin doctors)
> → Here is some advice from skin doctors.

1 여기 당신을 위한 또 다른 셔츠가 있다. (another shirt, for you)
→ ____________

2 여기 시험을 위한 몇 가지 요령이 있다. (some tips, for the exam)
→ ____________

3 여기 새로운 직원 명단이 있다. (a list of, the new employees)
→ ____________

**C** 우리말과 같은 뜻이 되도록 주어진 단어를 배열하여 문장을 완성하시오.

1 여드름은 청소년에게 큰 문제가 될 수 있다. (a big problem, be, acne, for teenagers, can)
→ ____________

2 순한 세안제로 세수해라. (your face, a mild cleanser, with, wash)
→ ____________

3 만약 여드름이 심각하다면, 피부과 전문의에게 진료를 받아라.
(a professional skin doctor, if, is, serious, see, your acne)
→ ____________

# 2 Culture

Chapter 5

**A** 영어는 우리말로, 우리말은 영어로 쓰시오.

1 province ____________
2 government ____________
3 tightly ____________
4 on duty ____________
5 put on ____________
6 엄격히 ____________
7 맞다, 적합하다 ____________
8 ~에 반대하여 ____________
9 목적 ____________
10 상기시키다 ____________

**B** 〈보기〉와 같이 우리말과 같은 뜻이 되도록 문장을 완성하시오.

보기 경찰은 그녀에게 긴 치마를 주었다. (the police officers, she, a long skirt)
→ The police officers gave her a long skirt.

1 여행 가이드는 우리에게 그 도시에 관한 정보를 주었다.
(the tour guide, we, some information, about the city)
→ ____________

2 그 선생님이 그녀에게 유익한 조언을 해 주었다. (the teacher, she, some helpful advice)
→ ____________

3 할아버지가 나에게 새 노트북 컴퓨터를 주셨다. (my grandpa, I, a new laptop)
→ ____________

**C** 우리말과 같은 뜻이 되도록 주어진 단어를 배열하여 문장을 완성하시오.

1 그들은 꼭 맞는 바지를 입을 수 없다. (cannot, tight pants, wear, they)
→ ____________

2 그들은 근무 중이다. (on, are, they, duty)
→ ____________

3 그녀는 설교사로부터 교육을 들어야 한다.(has to, a lesson, she, from a preacher, listen to)
→ ____________

# 3 Information

**A** 영어는 우리말로, 우리말은 영어로 쓰시오.

1 chew ______________
2 allow ______________
3 concentration ______________
4 steady ______________
5 carry out ______________
6 무례한, 예의 없는 ______________
7 방해하다 ______________
8 올리다 ______________
9 결과 ______________
10 긍정적인 ______________

**B** 〈보기〉와 같이 우리말과 같은 뜻이 되도록 문장을 완성하시오.

보기 껌을 씹는 것은 학생들이 더 높은 수학 점수를 받는 데 도움이 되는 것처럼 보였다.
(chewing gum, help, students, get better scores, in math)
→ Chewing gum seemed to help students get better scores in math.

1 학생들은 새로 오신 선생님을 좋아하는 것처럼 보였다. (the students, like, their new teacher)
→ ______________

2 그는 그 약속을 잊은 것처럼 보였다. (he, forget about, the appointment)
→ ______________

3 Jessie는 패션 디자인에 관심이 있는 것처럼 보였다. (Jessie, have an interest in, fashion design)
→ ______________

**C** 우리말과 같은 뜻이 되도록 주어진 단어를 배열하여 문장을 완성하시오.

1 어른들 앞에서 껌을 씹는 것은 무례하다고 여겨진다.
(to be rude, chewing gum in front of elders, is considered)
→ ______________

2 껌을 씹는 것이 학생들의 집중을 방해한다. (disturbs, chewing gum, students' concentration)
→ ______________

3 껌을 씹는 것이 집중에 긍정적인 영향을 끼친다. (a positive effect, chewing gum, on concentration, has)
→ ______________

# 4 Origin

Chapter 5

**A** 영어는 우리말로, 우리말은 영어로 쓰시오.

1 woods ______________

2 servant ______________

3 exactly ______________

4 beat on ______________

5 avoid ______________

6 그동안에 ______________

7 겁주다 ______________

8 관목, 덤불 ______________

9 ~에 들어가다 ______________

10 뛰쳐나가다 ______________

**B** 〈보기〉와 같이 우리말과 같은 뜻이 되도록 문장을 완성하시오.

보기 멧돼지들은 그들이 살았던 곳에서 달아났다. (the boars, ran out from, the place, they, lived)
→ The boars ran out from the place where they lived.

1 나는 아버지가 살았던 집에 방문했다. (I, visited, the house, my father, lived)
→ ______________________________

2 나는 그녀가 종종 쉬러 오는 곳으로 갔다. (I, go to, the place, she, often, takes a break)
→ ______________________________

3 Jason은 그가 신발을 샀던 그 가게로 갔다. (Jason, went to, the shop, he, bought, the shoes)
→ ______________________________

**C** 우리말과 같은 뜻이 되도록 주어진 단어를 배열하여 문장을 완성하시오.

1 그들은 나뭇가지를 두들겼다. (branches, they, beat on)
→ ______________________________

2 멧돼지들은 사람을 죽일 수 있다. (kill, boars, a man, can)
→ ______________________________

3 사냥꾼들은 그들을 쏘려고 했다. (tried to, them, the hunters, shoot)
→ ______________________________

# 1 Letters

Chapter 6

**A** 영어는 우리말로, 우리말은 영어로 쓰시오.

1 amazing ______________

2 jealousy ______________

3 get along with ______________

4 seem ______________

5 pity ______________

6 고집불통인 ______________

7 논쟁, 말다툼 ______________

8 공통점이 있다 ______________

9 밝게, 환하게 ______________

10 심술궂은 ______________

**B** 〈보기〉와 같이 우리말과 같은 뜻이 되도록 문장을 완성하시오.

보기 나는 그녀와 절대 어울릴 수 없을 거라고 말했다. (could, never, get along with, her)
→ I said I could never get along with her.

1 나는 회의에 늦을 거라고 말했다. (would, be, late for, the meeting)
→ ______________________________

2 나는 아프지 않다고 말했다. (wasn't, sick)
→ ______________________________

3 나는 내가 곧 일을 그만 둘 거라고 말했다. (would, quit, my job, soon)
→ ______________________________

**C** 우리말과 같은 뜻이 되도록 주어진 단어를 배열하여 문장을 완성하시오.

1 그녀는 심술궂고 고집불통인 것처럼 보였다. (seemed, she, mean and stubborn)
→ ______________________________

2 나는 종종 그녀와 말다툼을 하곤 했다. (often, arguments, I, with her, got into)
→ ______________________________

3 우리는 공통점이 많았다. (in common, we, a lot, had)
→ ______________________________

# 2 Psychology

Chapter 6

**A** 영어는 우리말로, 우리말은 영어로 쓰시오.

| | | | | | |
|---|---|---|---|---|---|
| 1 | responsibility | ______ | 6 | 이론 | ______ |
| 2 | likable | ______ | 7 | 참가자 | ______ |
| 3 | mess up | ______ | 8 | 지지하다 | ______ |
| 4 | now and then | ______ | 9 | 쏟다, 엎지르다 | ______ |
| 5 | knock over | ______ | 10 | 능력 | ______ |

**B** 〈보기〉와 같이 우리말과 같은 뜻이 되도록 문장을 완성하시오.

보기 누가 가장 높은 점수를 받았을까? (got, the highest score)
→ Who got the highest score?

1 누가 이 탁자를 옮길 수 있을까? (can, move, this table)
→ ______

2 누가 질문에 답할 수 있을까? (can, answer, the question)
→ ______

3 누가 지난밤에 그 경기에서 이겼을까? (won, the game, last night)
→ ______

**C** 우리말과 같은 뜻이 되도록 주어진 단어를 배열하여 문장을 완성하시오.

1 만약 내가 잘못하는 것이 하나도 없다면, 다른 사람들은 나를 더 좋아할 것이다.
(never do, if, anything wrong, I, others, me more, will like)
→ ______

2 누가 가장 높은 점수를 받았을까?(the, score, got, who, highest)
→ ______

3 사소한 실수를 하는 것이 완벽해지려고 노력하는 것보다 낫다.
(is, trying to be perfect, making little mistakes, better than)
→ ______

# 3 Science

Chapter 6

**A** 영어는 우리말로, 우리말은 영어로 쓰시오.

1 diet ______________
2 global warming ______________
3 fossil fuel ______________
4 endangered ______________
5 stomach ______________
6 나오다 ______________
7 실험실 ______________
8 많은 ______________
9 ~ 대신 ______________
10 줄이다 ______________

**B** 〈보기〉와 같이 우리말과 같은 뜻이 되도록 문장을 완성하시오.

보기 그것은 판다 위 안에 있는 특별한 물질 때문이다. (the special stuff, in panda's stomach)
→ It's because of the special stuff in panda's stomach.

1 그것은 과도한 업무 때문이다. (too much work)
→ ______________

2 그것은 나쁜 날씨 때문이다. (the bad weather)
→ ______________

3 그것은 교통 체증 때문이다. (a traffic jam)
→ ______________

**C** 우리말과 같은 뜻이 되도록 주어진 단어를 배열하여 문장을 완성하시오.

1 당분은 판다에게 모든 에너지를 제공한다. (gives, the panda, the sugar, all the energy)
→ ______________

2 특별한 물질이 판다의 배설물로 나온다. (comes out, in the panda's poop, special stuff)
→ ______________

3 우리는 화석 연료 대신에 대나무를 사용할 수 있다. (can, bamboo, we, use, fossil fuels, instead of)
→ ______________

# 4 Opinion

Chapter 6

**A** 영어는 우리말로, 우리말은 영어로 쓰시오.

1 blame ____________
2 planet ____________
3 nevertheless ____________
4 take care of ____________
5 make a mess of ____________
6 ~ 외에, 게다가 ____________
7 청소하다 ____________
8 붐비는 ____________
9 오염된 ____________
10 악화되다 ____________

**B** 〈보기〉와 같이 우리말과 같은 뜻이 되도록 문장을 완성하시오.

보기 나는 지구가 다소 위험하다고 생각해. (Earth, dangerous)
→ I think Earth is kind of dangerous.

1 나는 그 새 차가 다소 비싸다고 생각해. (the new car, expensive)
→ ____________

2 나는 그 문제가 다소 어렵다고 생각해. (the question, difficult)
→ ____________

3 나는 그 가방이 다소 무겁다고 생각해. (the bag, heavy)
→ ____________

**C** 우리말과 같은 뜻이 되도록 주어진 단어를 배열하여 문장을 완성하시오.

1 우리는 지구를 더 나은 곳으로 만들어야 한다. (a better place, need to, the world, we, make)
→ ____________

2 이 행성은 이미 오염되었다. (is, this planet, polluted, already)
→ ____________

3 너무 많은 자연 재해가 있다. (natural disasters, too, are, many, there)
→ ____________

# 1 Health

**A** 영어는 우리말로, 우리말은 영어로 쓰시오.

1 a bowl of ______________
2 fiber ______________
3 suggest ______________
4 nutritious ______________
5 fit ______________
6 시리얼 ______________
7 무기질 ______________
8 지방 ______________
9 놀라게 하다 ______________
10 맛있는 ______________

**B** 〈보기〉와 같이 우리말과 같은 뜻이 되도록 문장을 완성하시오.

> **보기** 당신은 현명한 소비자가 되어야 한다. (be, a smart shopper)
> → You have to be a smart shopper.

1 그들은 기차를 타기 위해 제 시간에 도착해야 한다. (arrive, on time, to catch, the train)
→ ______________________________

2 그는 다음 주 월요일까지 숙제를 끝내야 한다. (finish, his homework, by next Monday)
→ ______________________________

3 너는 난로 앞에서는 조심해야 한다. (be careful, in front of a heater)
→ ______________________________

**C** 우리말과 같은 뜻이 되도록 주어진 단어를 배열하여 문장을 완성하시오.

1 시리얼은 수백만 명의 사람들이 가장 좋아하는 아침 식사이다. (for millions, breakfast, favorite, is, cereal, a)
→ ______________________________

2 시리얼은 은밀한 비밀을 가지고 있다. (cereal, has, secret, dark, a)
→ ______________________________

3 몇몇 아침 식사용 시리얼은 당신의 건강에 좋다. (several breakfast cereals, are, you, good for,)
→ ______________________________

# 2 Letters

Chapter 7

**A** 영어는 우리말로, 우리말은 영어로 쓰시오.

1 review ________
2 especially ________
3 deaf ________
4 clever ________
5 feel left out ________
6 잡지 ________
7 건너뛰다 ________
8 다른 점에서는 ________
9 수화 ________
10 추천하다 ________

**B** 〈보기〉와 같이 우리말과 같은 뜻이 되도록 문장을 완성하시오.

보기 나는 그 책을 선생님께 추천했다. (the book, my teacher)
→ I recommended the book to my teacher.

1 나는 그 영화를 여동생에게 추천했다. (the movie, my sister)
→ ________

2 나는 그 자동차를 아버지께 추천했다. (the car, my father)
→ ________

3 나는 그 식당을 친구들에게 추천했다. (the restaurant, my friends)
→ ________

**C** 우리말과 같은 뜻이 되도록 주어진 단어를 배열하여 문장을 완성하시오.

1 나는 엄마에게 그 책에 대해 이야기했다. (the book, told, I, my mom, about)
→ ________

2 나는 가끔 소외감을 느끼고 외롭다. (often, and, feel left out, lonely, I)
→ ________

3 엄마가 나를 위해 그 책을 사 주셨다. (for me, my mom, the book, bought)
→ ________

# 3 Information

**A** 영어는 우리말로, 우리말은 영어로 쓰시오.

1 approve ________________

2 package ________________

3 calorie ________________

4 serving ________________

5 container ________________

6 상품, 제품 ________________

7 표, 라벨 ________________

8 함유하다 ________________

9 단백질 ________________

10 다르다 ________________

**B** 〈보기〉와 같이 우리말과 같은 뜻이 되도록 문장을 완성하시오.

> 보기 140 칼로리에 속지 마라. (be fooled by, the 140 calories)
>
> → Don't be fooled by the 140 calories.

1 질문하는 것을 두려워하지 마라. (be afraid, to ask a question)

→ ________________________________

2 내 공책을 가지고 오는 걸 잊지 마라. (forget, to bring, my notebook)

→ ________________________________

3 남동생을 더 이상 괴롭히지 마라. (bother, your brother, any more)

→ ________________________________

**C** 우리말과 같은 뜻이 되도록 주어진 단어를 배열하여 문장을 완성하시오.

1 라벨은 당신에게 식품에 무엇이 함유되어 있는지 정확히 알려준다.
(the food, the label, contains, tells you, exactly what)

→ ________________________________

2 1회분의 양은 제품에 따라 달라진다. (differs, the product, the serving size, depending on)

→ ________________________________

3 1회 제공량에 주의하라. (the serving size, attention, pay, to)

→ ________________________________

# 4 Science

Chapter 7

**A** 영어는 우리말로, 우리말은 영어로 쓰시오.

1 heat ______
2 flavor ______
3 pot ______
4 have to do with ______
5 straight away ______
6 온도 ______
7 섞이다 ______
8 끓다 ______
9 붓다, 따르다 ______
10 (전기, 가스 등을) 끄다 ______

**B** 〈보기〉와 같이 우리말과 같은 뜻이 되도록 문장을 완성하시오.

보기 물은 오래 끓일수록, 더 많은 공기가 잃게 된다. (long, the water, boil, much, it, lose, air)
→ The longer the water boils, the more it loses air.

1 많이 웃을수록, 더 행복하다. (much, you, smile, happy, you, be)
→ ______

2 어릴수록, 빨리 배운다. (young, be, fast, you, learn)
→ ______

3 방이 넓을수록 방세는 더 높다. (big, the room, be, high, the rent, be)
→ ______

**C** 우리말과 같은 뜻이 되도록 주어진 단어를 배열하여 문장을 완성하시오.

1 맛있는 차의 비결은 무엇일까? (a delicious cup of tea, the secret, to, what's)
→ ______

2 공기와 물은 낮은 온도에서 잘 섞인다. (mix together, at low temperatures, well, air and water)
→ ______

3 더 많은 공기를 가진 물은 차가 더 좋은 맛이 나도록 한다. (makes, taste better, water with more air, tea)
→ ______

# 1 Life

Chapter 8

**A** 영어는 우리말로, 우리말은 영어로 쓰시오.

1 relationship ______________
2 automatic ______________
3 small talk ______________
4 meaningful ______________
5 participant ______________
6 대화 ______________
7 분류하다 ______________
8 발견하다 ______________
9 행복 ______________
10 논의, 상의 ______________

**B** 〈보기〉와 같이 우리말과 같은 뜻이 되도록 문장을 완성하시오.

보기 그들은 가장 불행한 지원자들보다 의미 있는 대화 시간을 두 배 더 가졌다.
(had, many meaningful discussions, the unhappiest volunteers)
→ They had twice as many meaningful discussions as the unhappiest volunteers.

1 나는 친구보다 두 배 더 빨리 달렸다. (ran, fast, my friend)
→ ______________

2 그의 가방은 내 가방보다 두 배 더 크다. (is, big, mine)
→ ______________

3 Luke는 다른 학생들보다 두 배 더 열심히 공부했다. (studied, hard, other students)
→ ______________

**C** 우리말과 같은 뜻이 되도록 주어진 단어를 배열하여 문장을 완성하시오.

1 지원자들은 나흘 동안 자동 대화 녹음기를 착용했다.
(wore, for four days, automatic speech recorders, volunteers)
→ ______________

2 대화 양식에도 차이가 있었다. (a difference, there, in conversation styles, was)
→ ______________

3 행복은 혼자 보내는 시간이 적은 것과 깊은 관련이 있다. (relates strongly to, happiness, less time alone)
→ ______________

# 2 Health

Chapter 8

**A** 영어는 우리말로, 우리말은 영어로 쓰시오.

1 emotional ______________

2 improve ______________

3 workout ______________

4 disease ______________

5 release ______________

6 상쾌한 ______________

7 즉, 다시 말해서 ______________

8 주의가 흩어짐, 기분전환 ______________

9 해로운 ______________

10 관점 ______________

**B** 〈보기〉와 같이 우리말과 같은 뜻이 되도록 문장을 완성하시오.

보기 신 나게 웃은 후에 기분이 상쾌하지 않니? (refreshed, a good laugh)
→ Don't you feel refreshed after a good laugh?

1 운동한 후에 기분이 좋지 않니? (good, a workout)

→ ______________

2 숙면을 취한 후에 기분이 낫지 않니? (better, a good sleep)

→ ______________

3 다른 사람들을 도운 후에 기분이 행복하지 않니? (happy, helping other people)

→ ______________

**C** 우리말과 같은 뜻이 되도록 주어진 단어를 배열하여 문장을 완성하시오.

1 웃는 것이 건강을 나아지게 하는 데 어떻게 도움이 되는 걸까?
(does, how, laughing, to improve health, help)

→ ______________

2 그건 당신의 몸이 스트레스를 풀었기 때문이다. (your body, that's because, stress, released)

→ ______________

3 웃는 것은 좋은 운동이다. (good, is, workout, laughing, a)

→ ______________

# 3 Sports

## A 영어는 우리말로, 우리말은 영어로 쓰시오.

1 take over ____________
2 last ____________
3 around ____________
4 in action ____________
5 contain ____________
6 평균의 ____________
7 배회하다 ____________
8 방송 ____________
9 정말로, 사실은 ____________
10 차지하다 ____________

## B 〈보기〉와 같이 우리말과 같은 뜻이 되도록 문장을 완성하시오.

보기 그 경기들이 왜 그렇게 인기가 있는지 이해하기 어렵다. (the games)
→ It's hard to understand why the games are so popular.

1 그 식당이 왜 그렇게 인기가 있는지 이해하기 어렵다. (the restaurant)
→ ____________

2 그 강의가 왜 그렇게 인기가 있는지 이해하기 어렵다. (the lecture)
→ ____________

3 그 영화가 왜 그렇게 인기가 있는지 이해하기 어렵다. (the movie)
→ ____________

## C 우리말과 같은 뜻이 되도록 주어진 단어를 배열하여 문장을 완성하시오.

1 더 많은 사람들이 교회에 가기보다 미식축구 경기를 관람한다.
(watch NFL games, more people, go to church, than)
→ ____________

2 미식축구 중계는 실제 경기보다 더 많은 다시 보기로 되어 있다.
(has, the NFL broadcast, than, live play, more replays)
→ ____________

3 중계 방송은 스무 번의 광고 방송 시간을 포함한다. (includes, the broadcast, 20 commercial breaks)
→ ____________

# 4 Science

Chapter 8

**A** 영어는 우리말로, 우리말은 영어로 쓰시오.

1 probably ______________
2 obvious ______________
3 creatively ______________
4 focus on ______________
5 pay attention ______________
6 불가능한 ______________
7 방해하다 ______________
8 연결, 관련 ______________
9 ~로 이어지다 ______________
10 관련 없는 ______________

**B** 〈보기〉와 같이 우리말과 같은 뜻이 되도록 문장을 완성하시오.

> 보기 나는 집중하기 위해 노력했다. (pay attention)
> → I tried hard to pay attention.

1 나는 일찍 일어나기 위해 노력했다. (wake up, early)
→ ______________________________

2 나는 목적을 이루려고 노력했다. (achieve, my purpose)
→ ______________________________

3 나는 그를 도우려고 노력했다. (help, him)
→ ______________________________

**C** 우리말과 같은 뜻이 되도록 주어진 단어를 배열하여 문장을 완성하시오.

1 당신은 아침형 인간인가 아니면 저녁형 인간인가? (an evening person, a morning person, or, you, are)
→ ______________________________

2 지친 뇌는 한 가지에 쉽게 집중할 수 없다. (cannot, one thing, a tired brain, focus easily on)
→ ______________________________

3 생각들 사이의 평범하지 않은 결합은 창의력으로 이어진다.
(creativity, among ideas, the unusual connections, lead to)
→ ______________________________

# 1 People

Chapter 9

**A** 영어는 우리말로, 우리말은 영어로 쓰시오.

1 custom ______________
2 publish ______________
3 moral ______________
4 make fun of ______________
5 anonymously ______________
6 소설 ______________
7 시골의 ______________
8 엄격한 ______________
9 부드럽게, 완만하게 ______________
10 성공한 ______________

**B** 〈보기〉와 같이 우리말과 같은 뜻이 되도록 문장을 완성하시오.

보기 그녀는 마흔 한 살의 나이에 죽었다. (die)
→ She died at the age of 41.

1 그는 서른 살의 나이에 집을 샀다. (buy, a house)
→ ______________

2 그녀는 스무 살의 나이에 혼자 여행을 했다. (travel, alone)
→ ______________

3 그는 열다섯 살의 나이에 그 기계를 발명했다. (invent, the machine)
→ ______________

**C** 우리말과 같은 뜻이 되도록 주어진 단어를 배열하여 문장을 완성하시오.

1 그녀의 소설은 많은 영화로 만들어졌다. (many movies, her novels, have been made into)
→ ______________

2 그녀는 좀처럼 집에서 멀리 여행을 떠나지 않았다. (rarely, far, she, from home, traveled)
→ ______________

3 그녀의 일생 동안 소설 중 네 편만이 출판되었다.
(published during her lifetime, only four, her novels, of, were)
→ ______________

# 2 Health

**A** 영어는 우리말로, 우리말은 영어로 쓰시오.

1 regularly ______________
2 protect ______________
3 at least ______________
4 particularly ______________
5 association ______________
6 해로운, 유해한 ______________
7 긁다 ______________
8 휴식, 중단 ______________
9 칫솔 ______________
10 치아의 ______________

**B** 〈보기〉와 같이 우리말과 같은 뜻이 되도록 문장을 완성하시오.

보기 식사 후에 치아에 휴식을 주어야 한다는 것을 기억하라. (give, your teeth, a break, after meals)
→ Remember that you need to give your teeth a break after meals.

1 병 뚜껑을 다시 닫아 놓아야 한다는 것을 기억하라. (put, the lid, back, on the bottle)
→ ______________________________

2 창문을 닫아야 한다는 것을 기억하라. (close, the windows)
→ ______________________________

3 치과에 가야 한다는 것을 기억하라. (go, to, the dentist)
→ ______________________________

**C** 우리말과 같은 뜻이 되도록 주어진 단어를 배열하여 문장을 완성하시오.

1 이를 바로 닦는 것은 오히려 치아에 해를 끼친다. (more harm than good, brushing too soon, does)
→ ______________________________

2 이러한 음료엔 산이 많이 들어있다. (these drinks, acid, a lot of, have)
→ ______________________________

3 충분한 침을 만들기 위해 이렇게 많은 시간이 필요하다. (to make, you, enough saliva, need, this much time)
→ ______________________________

# 3 Economy

Chapter 9

**A** 영어는 우리말로, 우리말은 영어로 쓰시오.

| | | | |
|---|---|---|---|
| 1 guess | ____________ | 6 맛이 나다 | ____________ |
| 2 cost | ____________ | 7 평소처럼 | ____________ |
| 3 Switzerland | ____________ | 8 가격 | ____________ |
| 4 difference | ____________ | 9 정확히 | ____________ |
| 5 expensive | ____________ | 10 충분한 | ____________ |

**B** 〈보기〉와 같이 우리말과 같은 뜻이 되도록 문장을 완성하시오.

> **보기** 당신이 어디에 있든 그것들은 항상 같은 맛이다. (they, always, taste, the same)
> → No matter where you are, they always taste the same.

1 당신이 어디에 있든, 나를 잊지 마시오. (don't forget, me)
→ ____________________________________________

2 당신이 어디에 있든 인터넷을 사용할 수 있다. (you, can, use, the Internet)
→ ____________________________________________

3 당신이 어디에 있든 스스로를 잘 돌봐야 한다. (you, should, take care of, yourself)
→ ____________________________________________

**C** 우리말과 같은 뜻이 되도록 주어진 단어를 배열하여 문장을 완성하시오.

1 나는 가장 좋아하는 점심을 사러 밖으로 나갔다. (went out, I, my favorite, to buy, lunch)
→ ____________________________________________

2 그것은 완전히 똑같은 음식이다. (is, exactly, the same food, it)
→ ____________________________________________

3 당신이 점심을 사 먹기 위해 얼마가 필요한가? (need, you, how much, do, for your lunch)
→ ____________________________________________

# 4 Language

Chapter 9

**A** 영어는 우리말로, 우리말은 영어로 쓰시오.

1 confuse ____________

2 argument ____________

3 fight over ____________

4 encouragement ____________

5 remote control ____________

6 ~을 야기하다 ____________

7 모국의, 타고난 ____________

8 육체의, 신체의 ____________

9 줄여서, 생략하여 ____________

10 속이다, 기만하다 ____________

**B** 〈보기〉와 같이 우리말과 같은 뜻이 되도록 문장을 완성하시오.

> 보기 아이들이 가스레인지를 사용하도록 두지 마라. (use, gas stove)
> → Don't let children use gas stove.

1 아이들이 밤 늦게까지 놀도록 두지 마라. (hang out, late, at night)

→ ____________________

2 아이들이 컴퓨터 게임을 너무 많이 하도록 두지 마라. (play, computer games, too much)

→ ____________________

3 아이들이 식당에서 돌아다니도록 두지 마라. (run around, in the restaurant)

→ ____________________

**C** 우리말과 같은 뜻이 되도록 주어진 단어를 배열하여 문장을 완성하시오.

1 여기 우리를 혼란시키는 몇 개의 단어가 있다. (a few words, that, confuse, here are, us, words)

→ ____________________

2 몇몇 단어들은 같은 것을 의미하지 않는다. (mean, some words, don't, the same thing)

→ ____________________

3 수백 개의 영어 단어가 일상적인 한국어에서 사용된다.
(in everyday Korean, English words, are used, hundreds of)

→ ____________________

# 1 Art

**A** 영어는 우리말로, 우리말은 영어로 쓰시오.

1 unusual ____________
2 create ____________
3 paint ____________
4 dusty ____________
5 parking fee ____________
6 ~없이 ____________
7 붓 ____________
8 작품, 일 ____________
9 나타나다 ____________
10 ~을 두고 가다 ____________

**B** 〈보기〉와 같이 우리말과 같은 뜻이 되도록 문장을 완성하시오.

보기 사람들은 Rafael이 자신들의 자동차 위에 그림을 그려주길 원한다. (draw, on their cars)
→ People want Rafael to draw on their cars.

1 나는 네가 이 메시지를 그녀에게 전달해 주길 원한다. (deliver, this message, to her)
→ ____________

2 그는 내가 설거지하기를 원한다. (do the dishes)
→ ____________

3 그녀는 내가 자신의 생일을 기억해 주길 바란다. (remember, her birthday)
→ ____________

**C** 우리말과 같은 뜻이 되도록 주어진 단어를 배열하여 문장을 완성하시오.

1 Rafael과 그의 예술에는 뭔가 특이한 것이 있다. (about, Rafael and his art, something, there's, unusual)
→ ____________

2 Rafael은 먼지 사이로 손가락을 이리저리 움직인다. (his fingers, Rafael, around, in the dust, moves)
→ ____________

3 사람들은 주차장에 자신들의 먼지투성이 자동차를 두고 간다.
(their dusty cars, people, at the car park, leave)
→ ____________

# 2 Humor

Chapter 10

**A** 영어는 우리말로, 우리말은 영어로 쓰시오.

| | | | | | |
|---|---|---|---|---|---|
| 1 | plan | ______ | 6 | 도착하다 | ______ |
| 2 | ahead | ______ | 7 | 대신에 | ______ |
| 3 | by mistake | ______ | 8 | 동의하다 | ______ |
| 4 | type | ______ | 9 | 미망인, 과부 | ______ |
| 5 | the day before | ______ | 10 | 설교하다 | ______ |

**B** 〈보기〉와 같이 우리말과 같은 뜻이 되도록 문장을 완성하시오.

보기 나는 당신이 내려 오기를 몹시 바라고 있어요. (you, come down)
→ I can't wait for you to come down.

1 나는 여름이 오기를 몹시 바라고 있어요. (summer, come)
→ ______

2 나는 그 영화가 개봉하기를 몹시 바라고 있어요. (the movie, release)
→ ______

3 나는 그녀가 우리 가족을 방문하기를 몹시 바라고 있어요. (her, visit, my family)
→ ______

**C** 우리말과 같은 뜻이 되도록 주어진 단어를 배열하여 문장을 완성하시오.

1 그 부부는 호텔에서 만나기로 했다. (to, agreed, meet, at the hotel, the couple)
→ ______

2 그는 자신의 부인에게 간략한 이메일을 보냈다. (his wife, a quick email, to, sent, he)
→ ______

3 미망인은 이메일을 확인하고서 소리를 질렀다. (checked, and, the widow, screamed, her email)
→ ______

# 3 World News

**A 영어는 우리말로, 우리말은 영어로 쓰시오.**

1 local ____________
2 afloat ____________
3 inside ____________
4 rounded ____________
5 cut off ____________
6 조작하다, 조절하다 ____________
7 제거하다 ____________
8 살, 고기, 과육 ____________
9 힘 ____________
10 재배하다, 기르다 ____________

**B 〈보기〉와 같이 우리말과 같은 뜻이 되도록 문장을 완성하시오.**

> 보기 그 경주를 즐기는 방법을 배워보자. (enjoy, the race)
> → Let's learn how to enjoy the race.

1 알파벳을 읽는 방법을 배워보자. (read, alphabets)
→ ____________________

2 이 게임을 하는 방법을 배워보자. (play, this game)
→ ____________________

3 오븐을 사용하는 방법을 배워보자. (use, the oven)
→ ____________________

**C 우리말과 같은 뜻이 되도록 주어진 단어를 배열하여 문장을 완성하시오.**

1 그의 아버지는 엄청나게 큰 호박을 키웠다. (giant, his father, pumpkins, grew)
→ ____________________

2 당신은 호박의 과육을 모두 제거해야 한다. (all the flesh of the pumpkin, you, remove, have to)
→ ____________________

3 당신이 필요한 것은 많은 힘이다. (is, all you need, a lot of strength)
→ ____________________

# 4 Information

Chapter 10

**A** 영어는 우리말로, 우리말은 영어로 쓰시오.

1 beware of ____________
2 from now on ____________
3 had better ____________
4 pay attention to ____________
5 germ ____________
6 뚜껑 ____________
7 최근에 ____________
8 (변기의) 물을 내리다 ____________
9 폭발하다 ____________
10 보이지 않는 ____________

**B** 〈보기〉와 같이 우리말과 같은 뜻이 되도록 문장을 완성하시오.

보기 너는 변기의 뚜껑을 닫는 것이 좋겠다. (close, the toilet lid)
→ You had better close the toilet lid.

1 너는 지금 당장 병원에 가 보는 게 좋겠다. (see, a doctor, right now)
→ ____________

2 너는 택시를 타는 게 좋겠다. (take, a taxi)
→ ____________

3 너는 잠을 자러 가는 것이 좋겠다. (go, to sleep)
→ ____________

**C** 우리말과 같은 뜻이 되도록 주어진 단어를 배열하여 문장을 완성하시오.

1 너는 화장실을 깨끗하게 유지해야 한다. (keep, clean, you, your bathroom, must)
→ ____________

2 그는 사진을 찍기 위해서 특수한 카메라를 사용했다. (used, he, to take pictures, special cameras)
→ ____________

3 미세 세균들은 어디로든 간다. (eveywhere, go, tiny germs)
→ ____________

# 새 교과서 반영
# 중등 독해 시리즈
# READING 공감

- 최신 교과서의 학습 내용을 반영한 흥미롭고 유익한 스토리 구성
- 창의, 나눔, 문화, 건강, 과학, 심리, 음식, 직업 등의 다양한 주제
- 독해 실력 및 창의력을 향상시킬 수 있는 객관식, 서술형 문제 수록
- 세상에 이런 일이! 알면 알수록 재미있는 코너, 지식채널 수록
- 마인드맵을 활용한 단계별 스토리텔링 코너, 이미지맵 수록
- 어휘 실력을 탄탄하게 해 주는 코너, Review Test 수록
- 어휘, 문장 쓰기 실력을 향상시킬 수 있는 서술형 워크북 제공

NEXUS makes your next day
www.nexusEDU.kr | 책에 대해 궁금한 사항은 넥서스에듀 홈페이지 1:1 고객상담 게시판을 이용하세요.

| | 초1 | 초2 | 초3 | 초4 | 초5 | 초6 | 중1 | 중2 | 중3 | 고1 | 고2 | 고3 |
|---|---|---|---|---|---|---|---|---|---|---|---|---|
| Writing | | | | 공감 영문법+쓰기 1~2 | | | | | | | | |
| Writing | | | | | | 도전만점 중등내신 서술형 1~4 | | | | | | |
| Writing | | | | 영어일기 영작패턴 1-A, B · 2-A, B | | | | | | | | |
| Writing | | | | Smart Writing 1~2 | | | | | | | | |
| Reading | | | | | Reading 101 1~3 | | | | | | | |
| Reading | | | | | Reading 공감 1~3 | | | | | | | |
| Reading | | | | | This Is Reading Starter 1~3 | | | | | | | |
| Reading | | | | | | This Is Reading 전면 개정판 1~4 | | | | | | |
| Reading | | | | | This Is Reading 1-1 ~ 3-2 (각 2권; 총 6권) | | | | | | | |
| Reading | | | | | | 원서 술술 읽는 Smart Reading Basic 1~2 | | | | | | |
| Reading | | | | | | | | | 원서 술술 읽는 Smart Reading 1~2 | | | |
| Reading | | | | | | | | | [특급 단기 특강] 구문독해 · 독해유형 | | | |
| Listening | | | | | | Listening 공감 1~3 | | | | | | |
| Listening | | | | | The Listening 1~4 | | | | | | | |
| Listening | | | | | | After School Listening 1~3 | | | | | | |
| Listening | | | | | | 도전! 만점 중학 영어듣기 모의고사 1~3 | | | | | | |
| Listening | | | | | | | | | 만점 적중 수능 듣기 모의고사 20회 · 35회 | | | |
| TEPS | | | | | NEW TEPS 입문편 실전 250+ 청해 · 문법 · 독해 | | | | | | | |
| TEPS | | | | | | NEW TEPS 기본편 실전 300+ 청해 · 문법 · 독해 | | | | | | |
| TEPS | | | | | | | NEW TEPS 실력편 실전 400+ 청해 · 문법 · 독해 | | | | | |
| TEPS | | | | | | | | NEW TEPS 마스터편 실전 500+ 청해 · 문법 · 독해 | | | | |